Visions OF AMERICA
Visions OF THE CHURCH

We come with Joy and Peace
   for all Humanity.
   —paraphrase of Apollo 11

Timothy R. Harner, Esq.

TRUSTED
BOOKS
A DIVISION OF DEEP RIVER BOOKS

Contents

Visions of the Church: Peace and Joy

The Vision of America:

"We came in peace for all mankind."
Apollo 11

The Experience of America:

"Houston, we've had a problem."
Apollo 13

CHAPTER 1

The Great
Awakening

WHO DISCOVERED AMERICA?

WHO DISCOVERED AMERICA?
We used to say, "Christopher Columbus. In 1492, he sailed the ocean blue." Then we realized that Leif Ericsson reached North America in Viking ships centuries before Columbus reached the Caribbean in the Nina, the Pinta, and the Santa Maria.

Furthermore, speculation persists that voyagers from ancient civilizations—perhaps the Egyptians, or even explorers from fabled Atlantis—reached the Americas thousands of years ago. Then it occurred to us that Native Americans deserved the credit for discovering America. After all, they reached these shores millennia before anyone from Europe set sail!

As I grappled with how to begin this book without offending someone by my choice of who discovered America, it occurred to me that the true discoverers of America were not those who first saw America with their *eyes*. The true discoverers of America were those who first saw America with their *hearts*: Abraham, Moses and Jesus.

Abraham saw America when he left behind his homeland to seek a land where all people would be blessed. Moses saw America when he told Pharaoh to let his people go free.

Jesus saw America when he told us how to be good neighbors—Good Samaritans who bind the wounds of those in need even though we have been taught to hate them because of their race, their nation, or their religion.

Furthermore, Abraham, Moses and Jesus displayed the faith of all Americans—a faith in the future that kept them going no matter how bleak their lives became. Abraham kept going even when it looked as if he would never have a son to inherit his wealth. Moses kept going against a mighty Pharaoh even when he was an old, old man. And Jesus kept going even when he knew that He would have to die to save others.

CHRISTOPHER COLUMBUS

Americans love taking risks. And so Americans love—in the words of the popular introduction to *Star Trek*—"boldly going where no one has gone before." Perhaps that is why we so admire Christopher Columbus. He took a big risk. And he went boldly where—as far as he knew—no one had ever gone before.

Going back at least to the time of ancient Greece, we remember that some earnest scientific thinkers thoroughly believed that the world was round. Yet everyone continued *acting as if* the earth were flat. Columbus saw the practical application of the scientific speculation about a round-shaped earth. Boldy, he determined to try a new way to reach Asia by sailing *west* instead of, as was the common practice of his day, by sailing east.

This was a *risky* idea. No one knew what perils lay to the west.

This was a *bold* idea. No one had done it before.

So . . . Columbus boldly risked his life—and got "lost!" He ran into some islands that he thought were near India. In fact, he was still half a world away from India. He was in the Caribbean Islands, only a short distance from the American mainland.

Columbus not only proved that the world was round—he proved that, when we take bold risks, even our failures can become successful beyond our wildest dreams.

Following in the footsteps of Columbus, Americans love to take risks. Americans love to boldly go where no one has gone before—to do things that no one has ever done before. Why? Because Americans are confident that—when we take bold risks to do new things—even our "failures" can become successful beyond our wildest dreams.

GOD, GOLD, AND GLORY

Unfortunately, when we take bold risks to do new things, we sometimes stir up more trouble than our worst nightmares. And the results of Christopher Columbus's voyages soon led to nightmares that plague us to this day.

The first nightmare was a personal one for Christopher Columbus. When his next voyages failed to reach India, i.e., failed to make an immediate profit, he soon became poor and socially despised.

But the most lasting nightmares afflicted the Native Americans and the Native Africans. Before long, they too became poor and despised.

Other Europeans soon followed Columbus to the New World, seeking—as we were taught when I was in elementary school, "God, Gold, and Glory." The advanced weaponry of the Europeans crushed empires in the New World that had flourished for centuries. And the religious zeal of the conquerors obliterated native cultures. Despair and disease exacerbated the horrors of being conquered by these alien overlords.

Seeking to exploit new sources of wealth, the Europeans needed even more workers. So they enslaved Native Africans and brought them to this torturous New World. In the short run, immense profits were the fruit of this cruelty. But in the long run, the results were disastrous for Africa and the Americas.

In Africa, the chaos brought the downfall of empires that had flourished for centuries. And in America, man's cruel inhumanity to man spread the blight of racism, marring the landscape of daily life. In these ways, the New World of the conquistadors became a waking nightmare of epic proportions.

THE FIRST AMERICANS: THE NATIVE AMERICANS

Just as there are many ways to answer the question "Who discovered America?" there are many ways to answer the question "Who were the first Americans?" One good way to answer this question is to say, "The Native Americans." They were the first people to settle North and South America. They migrated to these continents thousands of years before Columbus. So they were indeed the first Americans in terms of chronology.

In many ways they are also the "first" Americans in the sense of being those people who have struggled mightily. They have known what it means to struggle against invaders who are superior in military power and superior in technology. They have known what it means to struggle for centuries, even as the triumphant invaders treated them with contempt.

And in many ways they are also the "first" Americans in the sense of being the people who most cherish nature. One reason the Native Americans lost North America to the European invaders was that Native Americans simply could not understand how any *one* human being could claim to own the land, the forests, the animals, the fish, the water, and the air. From their perspective, these were gifts from God for all to share.

Long before modern Americans saw pictures of the earth from space and realized that we must protect our little oasis in space— or realized that no national boundaries or property lines divide our world the way that God sees it—Native Americans understood such truths. In this, and in all these other ways, Native Americans were *the first Americans*.

The First Americans: The Africans

Another group of people who can lay claim to being the "first" Americans were the people who came from Africa. For over a century, the New World was dominated by the Spanish and the Portuguese. They soon learned that Africans made excellent slaves in hot, tropical climates. The blight of slavery, however, did not reach the lands that became the United States of America due to the Spanish or the Portuguese. Slavery reached these lands due to the English.

In 1588, the English defeated the Spanish Armada. After that naval victory, control of the oceans—and control of the lands that lay beyond the oceans in America, Africa, and Asia—began to pass to the new master of the waves: England.

In 1607 the first permanent English colony was established in the New World at Jamestown. This colony struggled for survival until it produced a crop that could be exported to Europe at a profit: tobacco. Henceforth, more labor was needed to make more money exporting the crop.

To meet this need, Africans—and people descended from Africans—were brought to Jamestown. The first slaves arrived in Jamestown in 1619.

These "first Americans" drained swamps, grew crops, and built houses. At the crack of a whip, from dawn to dusk they proved that only hard work could tame this New World. So, in the sense of those working hardest to carve out a new frontier, *they* were the "first" Americans.

They were also the "first" Americans in the sense of being foremost in the struggle for freedom and human dignity. As we shall see, Americans have always struggled for freedom and human dignity. From the embattled farmers at Lexington and Concord to Americans raising the Star-Spangled Banner in victory during World War II, they have struggled. From Roger Williams demanding religious freedom to Susan B. Anthony demanding the right to vote, they have struggled. In the establishment of the American way of life, struggle is a constant theme.

But none of these struggles has been as long or as frustrating as the struggle of Africans for their rights and privileges as Americans. Africans suffered the cruelty of slavery for 244 years—from their arrival at Jamestown until the Emancipation Proclamation of 1863. Even after gaining their legal freedom, they suffered from the degradation of segregation for 100 years more—until the Civil Rights victories of the 1960s. Often, they still suffer from racism to this day.

We honor runners who win 100-meter sprints. But we stand in awe of those who win 26-mile marathons. In a similar way, we honor those who struggled for *years* with George Washington to defend their right to life, liberty, and the pursuit of happiness. But we stand in awe of those who struggled for *centuries*—and who struggle still—to make the vision of a free America a reality.

THE FIRST AMERICANS: THE PILGRIMS

Obviously, the English were starting down the same path of misery and exploitation in the New World that the Spanish and the Portuguese had long traveled. Tobacco has sickened the bodies of untold numbers of people. And slavery has sickened the spirits of countless numbers of people.

Yet such cornerstones of horror laid the foundation for English "success" in the New World. Certainly, the odds were against the Pilgrims, who sailed from Plymouth, England, in a small ship in 1620, about one year after the first Africans arrived at Jamestown. These "first" Americans were small in number, but large in vision. And their ultimate success was certain.

Why? Because these *Pilgrims* did not seek gold or glory in America. The Pilgrims sought God, and their vision of America did not tempt people to become enslaved to the false gods of gold or glory.

Their vision of America inspired people to live the way that Jesus lived: loving the Lord our God with all of our heart, soul, and mind, and loving our neighbor as ourselves. The Pilgrim vision of America did not measure success by how much gold or glory they could boast about.

Their vision of America measured success by how fully their lives bore the fruit of the Holy Spirit: love, joy, peace, patience, kindness, goodness, faithfulness, gentleness, and self-control.

VISIONS OF AMERICA

So by 1620, the three greatest forces for good in the New World—the three best visions of America—were in place: the vision of the Native Americans, the vision of the Africans and the vision of the Pilgrims. These three visions were to meld into a force for change and growth that is recognized today as uniquely and indigenously *American*. How this happened is the fascinating subject of the book you now hold in your hands.

Native Americans lived in the *Land of the Free* by seasonally roaming a "Garden of Eden," replete with mighty rivers, pristine mountains, and towering forests "from sea to shining sea." They symbolize the need to be "good gardeners" of the Good Earth[1] that God has given us.

The Africans began their courageous fight for human dignity and economic justice—effectively shaping this New World into the *Home of the Brave*. They symbolize the need to end the curse that started with the first sin in the Garden of Eden—the curse that says "thorns" will choke out the work of our hands as we struggle vainly to produce useful crops by the sweat of our brows. And they symbolize the need to overcome the curse of the Tower of Babel—the communications curse that insisted that racial and national hatreds would prevent us from being all that we could be.

The Pilgrims risked everything to live in a way that was pleasing to God—a way of life in which we love God and in which we treat other people the same way that we want to be treated. They symbolize the need to *boldly go where no one has gone before* to establish a New World of "Good Samaritans."

In this New World, even the most despised person—such as the Samaritan woman whom Jesus met at a well (John 4:4–42)—

might worship God "in spirit and in truth." And in this New World, Good Samaritans would help all of their neighbors—regardless of whether those neighbors were of a different religion, race, or nationality.

ROGER WILLIAMS AND "RELIGIOUS FREEDOM"

One of the first "Good Samaritans" of America was Roger Williams. He led the way in establishing religious freedom in America.

Roger Williams was constantly at loggerheads with the Puritans of the Massachusetts Bay colony. The Puritans wanted to purify the Church of England, but they did not want to stop using the power of the government to raise money for the church. Nor did they want to stop forcing people to attend the government's churches. They felt strongly that forcing wicked people to hear the Word of God was the best way to encourage them to become Christians.

Roger Williams believed exactly the opposite. How could people love God freely if they were *forced* to follow him? Williams argued that the government should stop forcing people to give money to support one church and that the government should stop forcing people to attend church. Instead, the government should play the same role as the captain on a ship. The government should guarantee the right of each "passenger on the ship" to worship God in the way in which that passenger thought best. This idea he called "religious freedom."

Religious *freedom* is a far better idea than mere religious *toleration*.

To say that we will "tolerate" something means that we will permit it to exist even though we don't like it or it is bad. *Religious toleration* was a vast improvement over the *religious intolerance* that marked the religious wars and persecutions that tormented Europe after the Protestant Reformation. But *religious freedom* is far superior. Why?

Religious freedom springs from a realization that in order to love the LORD our God with all our heart, soul, and mind, we must be *free* to love. We cannot force people to love God any more than we can force a man and a woman to fall in love with each other. Indeed, trying to *force* a man and a woman to fall in love with each other is one of the best ways to make sure that they *never* fall in love with each other!

Religious freedom also takes away the tyrannical pretense of governments as "all powerful." Indeed, it is far more important that we love the LORD our God and that we love our neighbors as ourselves than that we love our nation (or any other human institution). So, as we affirm every time that we pledge allegiance to the flag of the United States of America, nations are *under* God, and nations (and other human institutions) do *not* have the right to dictate what people think or believe.

In the 1630s and 1640s, such radical ideas led Roger Williams to flee the tyranny of the Puritans in Massachusetts and to found a new colony where true *religious freedom* was practiced: Rhode Island. It was a grand experiment that ultimately proved successful.

By "boldly going where no one had gone before" in promoting religious freedom, Roger Williams took a giant leap forward for all humanity.

THE GREAT AWAKENING

The awakening of religious freedom in America was not the only Great Awakening that took place in the New World. About a century after the Pilgrims landed at Plymouth Rock and after Roger Williams began practicing religious freedom, a series of religious revivals known as the Great Awakening swept through the English colonies of the Eastern seaboard. The tone of these revivals sounds almost strange to today's Christian:

"The best-known and most brilliant leader of 'The Great Awakening' was Jonathan Edwards, who claimed that he 'made seeking salvation the main business of [his] life.' And no wonder! Jonathan Edwards 'preached that God was a pitiless being before whom man was helpless; that God rejoiced in suspending

19

man 'over the pit of Hell much as one holds a spider or some loathsome insect over the fire.'"[1]

This image of sinners suspended over "a great furnace of wrath, a wide and bottomless pit, full of the fire of wrath" comes from one of his most famous sermons: "Sinners in the Hands of an Angry God." In this sermon, Jonathan Edwards stressed such themes as "the fierceness and wrath of *Almighty* God." For example, he warned each person sitting in the church that "[t]here will be no end to this exquisite, horrible misery" because even after you have actually spent "millions of millions of ages, in wrestling and conflicting with this almighty, merciless vengeance . . . you will know that all is but a point to what remains. So that your punishment will indeed be infinite."[2]

Such *hellfire and brimstone* sermons were far different in tone from the preaching of the greatest evangelist of the Twentieth Century, Billy Graham. Although Billy Graham warns people about the danger of eternal damnation, the main theme of his preaching is the Good News that "God so loved the world that he gave his one and only son, Jesus Christ, so that whoever believes in him shall not perish but have eternal life" (John 3:16).

Nevertheless, this Great Awakening of Christians in the English colonies nurtured a vision of America that was worthy of a New World. Americans learned that they must bear every burden and meet every hardship[3] to be who God wants them—indeed, who God *demands* them—to be: people who "love the Lord our God with all our heart and with all our soul and with all our mind" (Matthew 22:37); and people who "love our neighbor as ourselves" (Matthew 22:39).

There is no contradiction between such a religious vision of America and religious freedom *in* America. Maintaining a society that allows for religious freedom is the best way to follow Jesus' command to treat other people the way that we want to be treated.

Religious freedom is also necessary because love for God and love for people can only arise from free will. Love cannot be created by coercion. And religious freedom is wise because the private sector is better at operating a church than is any public government.

Upholding religious freedom is the best way to achieve the mission of Christianity: to go and make disciples of all humanity (Matthew 28:19–20) so that they produce the fruit of the Holy Spirit: love, joy, peace, patience, kindness, goodness, faithfulness, gentleness, and self-control (Galatians 5:22–23).

Only such *Great Awakenings* as Roger Williams had can fulfill the vision of America first seen by Abraham, Moses, and Jesus—a vision of an America that is not limited to the "United States of America." This vision of an ideal America guides anyone who seeks a "New World" where people will love God with all their heart and with all their soul and with all their mind . . . and where people will love their neighbor as themselves.

Abraham envisioned such an "America"—such a "Promised Land"—where all people would be blessed. Moses envisioned such an "America," where all people would be set free to find the "Promised Land." And Jesus envisioned such an "America," where all people would be good neighbors—Good Samaritans—who bind the wounds of those in need even though they have been taught to hate them because of their race, their nation, or their religion.

Only such *Great Awakenings* can sustain the faith of all Americans—a faith in the future that keeps us going no matter how bleak the present may sometimes be. Abraham found faith to keep going even when it looked as if he would never have an heir to inherit his name and his wealth. And by faith he knew that his greatest "wealth" was his dream of a "Promised Land" that God was leading him toward, one where *all* people and nations would be blessed.

Moses found the faith to keep going against a mighty Pharaoh, even when he was a very old man. And Jesus found faith to keep going even when he was called upon to give His life to save others. Only such Great Awakenings can enable Americans to come together in peace for the sake of all humanity.

BENJAMIN FRANKLIN

Religion was not the only realm in which colonial America began to awaken. Benjamin Franklin himself epitomized the first awakenings of the power of the press, the power of science, and the power of technology in America.

Franklin rose to fame as the author of *Poor Richard's Almanack*. Using the power of the press, he popularized many sayings that captured the hardy spirit of the times, such as: "Early to bed and early to rise, makes a man healthy, wealthy and wise" and "God helps them that help themselves."

His most famous scientific experiment was putting a key on a kite during a lightning storm in order to prove that lightning was electricity. He could easily have been electrocuted, which showed that Americans were still as bold and reckless in their search for new knowledge as when Christopher Columbus sailed across uncharted waters in search of India.

Benjamin Franklin, with his practical frame of mind, was not content writing clever words and discovering bits and pieces of scientific truth. With an engineer's passion for technology, he used science to help people. He helped people keep warm with his pot-bellied stove. And he helped people see better with his bifocals.

Benjamin Franklin's inquiring, questioning mind did not stop with science and technology. He also doubted and questioned the scientific and historical underpinnings of Christianity. Moreover, his numerous affairs with women flaunted his disregard for puritanical morality.

And so, even from these earliest times, the press, the scientists, and the engineers created zest and controversy along with their new ideas, new discoveries, and new inventions. You can't make an omelet without breaking a few eggs. And you can't "boldly go where no one has gone before" without changing the way people think and changing the way people behave.

As Jesus explained to the Pharisees–the puritanical people of his time who preferred to keep their traditions instead of helping people: "You can't pour new wine into old wineskins. If you do, the old wineskins will burst, ruining both the wineskins and the wine" (Matthew 9:17).

A New World is the ultimate "new wine skin." So Americans such as Benjamin Franklin eagerly—if irreverently at times—set about filling their New World with the "new wine" of America: new ideas and practices never before seen on this planet!

LEXINGTON AND CONCORD

It was not long before the "new wine" of America burst the "old wineskins" of the British Empire. It happened at two small New England towns: Lexington and Concord.

For more than 150 years after the founding of the first English colony in North America at Jamestown, the colonies had been dependent on the motherland economically and militarily. Therefore, despite tensions from time to time, there was no serious effort to establish a separate nation in America.

This period of dependency began to change after 1763 when the British Empire won a "world war" against the French that had been simmering off-and-on for generations. The peace treaty ending the war drove the French out of North America, giving Britain control of Canada. Now the English colonies no longer feared French subjugation.

The American colonists were eager to exploit the vast wealth that lay to the west. But the British Empire did not care as much about making Americans rich and powerful. Instead, the British were reluctant to stir up Indian wars through rapid expansion westward. Furthermore, the British were interested in having the American colonists pay the huge war debt that had accumulated during the recently concluded "world war." Indeed, there was some justice in the British demand because Britain had expended much money and many lives driving the French out of North America.

However, the people paying the taxes rarely view things the same way as the people receiving the taxes. And Americans were no exception.

Tensions rose and fell for about a decade. Britain would impose taxes on the colonists. The colonists would complain about the taxes. The British would use harsher and harsher ways to enforce the taxes. The colonists would complain about the harshness of British authority. Britain would reduce the taxes, but would never eliminate them entirely.

Despite American protests that they could not be forced to pay taxes that their colonial legislatures had never imposed, the British were adamant that they had the power to impose taxes on the colonists. The British made a serious miscalculation after one of the American outbursts against taxation without representation: the Boston Tea Party.

Boston had long been a hotbed of resistance to British authority. Indeed, New England's Yankees followed in a long line of king-haters that stretched back more than a century—to the Puritans who fled England to escape religious and political persecution under King Charles the First. Many of these Puritans settled in Boston and surrounding towns, such as Salem.

Back in England in the 1620s and 1630s, the Puritans and King Charles the First were constantly at loggerheads over politics and religion. King Charles tried to weaken the power of Parliament and the Puritans tried to strengthen the power of Parliament. Since the King desperately needed money, many of the struggles involved the King trying to impose taxes without Parliament's consent. These struggles between the Puritans and King Charles culminated in the English Civil War during the 1640s.

The amount of time that separated the fighting at Lexington and Concord from the fighting during the English Civil War is about the same that separates us from the struggle to free the slaves during the American Civil War. So, the lessons that the English learned about defending their lives, liberties, and property in the English Civil War would have been as meaningful to the American farmers who fought at Lexington and Concord as the lessons that Americans learned about defending "Life, Liberty, and the Pursuit of Happiness" in the American Civil War are to us.

King Charles the First came to the throne in 1625. He believed in the principle: *a deo rex, a rege lex*—"The king is from God, and law from the king." In other words, King Charles believed in the "divine-right" of kings. Therefore, he strove to rid himself of the interference of Parliament as much as possible.

But the Puritans (who were primarily from the rising "middle class" of England) relied on Parliament to promote their interests and to protect their lives, liberties, and property. For example, in 1628, using its "Power of the Purse," Parliament compelled the cash-strapped king to sign the Petition of Right. This law guaranteed English subjects basic rights, such as freedom from taxation without Parliament's consent.

The struggle between King Charles and the Puritans also involved the explosive issue of religion. As the head of the Church of England, King Charles believed that keeping his throne safe depended on keeping the Church of England strong. But the Puritans constantly attacked "popish" practices and beliefs of the Church of England. Indeed, they were known as "Puritans" because they wanted to "purify" the Church of England from all traces of Catholicism.

At first, it appeared that King Charles would succeed in stamping out Parliament and the Puritans. Charles dissolved Parliament in 1629 and ruled without calling a new Parliament until 1640—more than an entire decade. He stretched the power of the monarchy to the maximum in order to raise money without having to ask Parliament for consent.

During this dark, discouraging time, the Puritans looked for a refuge from political and religious tyranny. And their eyes turned to the new lands of New England. Therefore, these stubborn, independent-minded people sailed to Massachusetts in large numbers, forever shaping the character and destiny of New England.

By 1640, King Charles became so desperate for money that he had to call Parliament back into session. (Scotland had rebelled against England because of a religious controversy that was sparked when King Charles tried to impose a new Prayer Book on Scottish churches, and King Charles did not have enough money to raise an army to defeat the Scots who—with the encouragement of the Puritans—invaded England.)

Parliament made sure that never again would there be any question about a fundamental safeguard of English liberties and property—no tax could be imposed without the consent of Parliament.

Or, as the Americans phrased it when they fought against the power of England to tax them without the consent of their colonial legislatures—their colonial "Parliaments": *No taxation without representation!*

These safeguards of "English liberties"—today we would call them "human rights"—had to be preserved on the battlefield. Within two years, civil war broke out between Parliament and King Charles. King Charles lost. In 1649 the Puritans executed him.

For the next 11 years (until "the Restoration" of the monarchy in 1660), England had no king. England was a "republic" (it would be more accurate to call it a "military dictatorship") ruled by Oliver Cromwell, the victorious general of the Puritan armies.[1]

This culmination of the struggle between the Puritans and King Charles did not bode well for King George III being able to convince Massachusetts to yield peacefully to his rule and to British taxes.

The fighting at Lexington and Concord was the result of British over-reaction to the Boston Tea Party. During this most famous "tea party" in history, a group of Bostonians protested the British tax on tea by tossing a ship's cargo of tea into Boston Harbor.

Far away in London, the outraged, haughty, arrogant rulers of the British Empire miscalculated horribly. To teach these despised colonists better manners, King George III imposed draconian measures that fueled American fears and anger. For example, the British closed Boston Harbor and occupied Boston with their troops.

The descendants of the Puritans in New England did not meekly submit to the tyranny of King George the Third any more than their Puritan ancestors had submitted to the tyranny of King Charles the First. British troops in Boston began to fear for their safety. So, in a "preemptive strike," the British commander in Boston, General Gage, tried to launch a surprise attack that would destroy American military supplies.

However, it was impossible to surprise the Americans. Patriots were everywhere, spying out the British plans for a quick march through Lexington to capture military supplies at Concord.

The drama of those days is captured best in Henry Wadsworth Longfellow's epic poem, *The Midnight Ride of Paul Revere*. The poem begins with the famous lines:

Listen, my children, and you shall hear,
Of the midnight ride of Paul Revere.

The cleverness of signaling Paul Revere by hanging lanterns in the steeple of Old North Church is memorialized in these classic lines:

One if by land, and two if by sea;
And I on the opposite shore will be,
Ready to ride and spread the alarm
Through every Middlesex village and farm.

And the importance of that fight for liberty was underscored in the realization that:

The fate of a nation was riding that night.

In fact, no one understood just how memorable the events of the next day would be. Because coincidence was as important as courage in choosing this moment and this place for the "Great Awakening" of the American Revolution. Just as Columbus discovered America by mistake, these first American soldiers began the fight for American independence by mistake.

The townspeople (mostly farmers) who answered the early morning call to muster at the village green in Lexington were extremely courageous to stand up against trained British soldiers. Nevertheless, they might well have marched away rather than offering battle, except that a shot rang out, leading to answering volleys that began the armed conflict. Although no one has ever been certain who fired the first shot, it is far more likely that the undisciplined Americans fired a stray bullet than that the trained British troops made such an error.

The agrarian townspeople's militia at Concord did not even try to prevent the British from entering the town. But when the British began burning some plunder, the Americans mistakenly thought that their homes were being burned. So they plucked up their courage, drove the British from an arched wooden bridge, and marched into history and glory.

This *Great Awakening* of the America Revolution is best captured in the famous words of the poem *A Shot Heard 'Round the World*, penned by Ralph Waldo Emerson:

By the rude bridge that arched the flood,
Their flag to April's breeze unfurled,
Here once the embattled farmers stood,
And fired the shot heard 'round the world.

THE DECLARATION OF INDEPENDENCE

Things went from bad to worse for the British during the first year of the American Revolution. After facing the fury of the embattled farmers at Concord, the British realized what a hornet's nest they'd stirred up. In those days, men hunted regularly to feed their families. As word spread about the British attack, more and more men started hunting the British troops as they retreated towards Boston. Taking cover behind rocks, trees and fences, these embattled farmers almost turned the British retreat into a rout.

Once the British made it back to Boston, they never again tried such a raid into the countryside. In Boston, they soon found themselves surrounded by multitudes of angry, armed Americans.

To maintain access to the sea, the British attacked American troops dug in at Bunker Hill. Although the British eventually captured the position because the Americans ran out of ammunition, the stiff resistance against Britain's best troops—and heavy British casualties—raised American hopes and British fears.

Other colonies sent help, including a commanding general who became the father of the new nation: George Washington. As would become habitual throughout the Revolution, George Washington faced the daunting task of commanding raw troops who lacked adequate supplies and ammunition. Nevertheless, Washington kept Boston besieged until the British army sailed away to Canada in March, 1776, almost a year after the fighting began at Lexington and Concord.[1]

For a period of several months, there was essentially no British military presence in the rebellious colonies. During these happy days, the elated colonists decided to take the decisive step of becoming an independent nation.

As the Continental Congress in Philadelphia debated what to do, Thomas Jefferson played a leading role in drafting a bold "Declaration of Independence." If you read the entire document penned by Jefferson, you can see that he used every argument imaginable to justify the extraordinary step toward independence that colonial American leaders had determined to make. This was not a mere revolt against a particular king—as the Puritans had revolted against King Charles. Casting about for a political theory to justify the creation of a new nation, Jefferson hit upon using popular ideas about "natural law" that were simultaneously stirring all of Europe.

In particular, Jefferson borrowed an idea from the British political theorist, John Locke. Locke had talked about a theoretical "state of nature" that existed before there was any government. He argued that government was a contract between itself and the people that was agreed to in this "state of nature." However, said Locke, there were some rights that were so intrinsic and precious that they could not be bargained away in any contract. These rights were "unalienable"—an archaic legal term that meant that something could not be sold.[2]

Locke drew his ideas from Britain's Glorious Revolution of 1688. The "Glorious Revolution" was a peaceful coup d'etat. The English Civil War had been fought a generation before, and few people wanted to revisit the turmoil and carnage of those days. So when the English king, James II, created a standing army (reminiscent of the Puritan Army that maintained Cromwell's dictatorship) and when James II (who was Catholic) seemed to be trying to make

England a Catholic country, all of the powerful forces in England united against him.

They invited William of Orange, the leader of the Netherlands and of the Protestant cause in Europe, to become their monarch—together with his English queen, Mary. When William and his army arrived in England, the English nation and the English army deserted James and proclaimed William and Mary their rulers.[3]

To justify this coup d'etat, Locke reasoned that once the government broke its "contract" with the people it governed, the people could protect their rights by entering into a new contract with a new government. Jefferson did not have to stretch far to use such reasoning to justify forming a new nation: the United States of America.

Jefferson did, however, want a more pleasing way of stating the idea than Locke had used. Locke had talked about the right to life, liberty and property. Jefferson decided that the phrase "the pursuit of happiness" had a better ring to it than the word "property."

Jefferson passed his first draft of the Declaration of Independence to other Founding Fathers for their review. He was irked at the many changes that they made. But the key passage survived . . . the passage where the *Great Awakening of America* took literary form—words heard round the world that gave meaning to the shots of the embattled farmers of Lexington and Concord . . . the passage where America declared "these truths to be self-evident, that . . ."

> [A]ll men are created equal; [and] are endowed by their Creator with certain unalienable rights; [and] that among these [rights] are life, liberty, and the pursuit of happiness.

CHAPTER 2

We the People

WASHINGTON CROSSES THE DELAWARE

NO SOONER HAD THE LIBERTY BELL stopped ringing the good news about American independence than Americans started wringing their hands at how badly the war was going.[1] A key reason for declaring independence was the hope that France and other European powers who disliked England would send help to America. But no European help came. Instead, the Europeans waited to see if America could survive the British onslaught that soon began.

When the British attacked, they struck at New York City, humiliating America's ill-trained, ill-equipped troops. As usual, George Washington was better at retreating and at holding his ragtag army together than at winning battles. He abandoned New York City, fleeing into New Jersey, and the jubilant British felt that victory was certain. But their arrogant overconfidence became their undoing.

As Winston Churchill later observed, if the British had pursued Washington as doggedly after the Americans lost New York City as Grant pursued Lee after the Confederates lost Richmond, the American Revolution might have ended in 1776 within a few months after the Declaration of Independence.[2] But the cocky British did not pursue the retreating Americans vigorously.

British sloth was matched by British foolishness. When the British took up their winter quarters, they recklessly scattered some of their troops among several towns in New Jersey. In their arrogance, they never dreamt that the whipped Americans would turn and attack the "British" outposts. (Many of the troops being used by the British were mercenaries—professional soldiers from Germany, called Hessians, who would fight for whoever paid them.)

Most of all, the British did not know that George Washington was the kind of person—and that America was the kind of nation—that never gives in. On Christmas Eve, Washington gambled the survival of his army and the survival of America on a desperate attack across the icy waters of the Delaware River.

Washington's military objective was to destroy the British/ Hession troops at Trenton. His political objective was to inspire America to continue to fight for independence. His daring victory achieved both objectives.

We've all seen the painting of Washington standing tall in a boat surrounded by "icebergs" as he crossed the Delaware. The artist took liberty with the physical facts, but he captured the symbolic truth about Washington's desperate attack. "Icebergs" of disaster threatened America's survival. And Washington never stood taller than when he refused to be cowed by a string of humiliating defeats and retreats, but instead retained enough confidence in his troops and in his cause to attack.

Such miracles of courage are rare in life—and in warfare. As a top German General wrote about the French counterattack at the Marne River early in World War I that saved France from defeat and became known as the "Miracle of the Marne":

> That men will let themselves be killed where they stand, that is
> a well-known thing and counted on in every plan of battle. But
> that men who have retreated [again and again], sleeping on the
> ground and half dead with fatigue, should be able to take up
> their rifles and attack when the bugle sounds, is a thing upon

which we never counted. It was a possibility not studied in our war academy.[3]

Nor was the possibility of such a miracle of courage studied in the British "war academy" before the American Revolution. General Washington and the American Army exceeded all expectations when the bugle sounded—when their Vision of America beckoned—and they crossed the Delaware.

VALLEY FORGE

By standing tall and trying again despite repeated failures, George Washington rose to the level of glory attained only by those, such as Winston Churchill, who persevere despite setbacks and incredible odds against them. Such people pass the test of character set by Churchill himself:

"Never give in! Never give in! Never, Never, Never, Never—in nothing great or small, large or petty. Never give in, except to convictions of honour and good sense."[1]

Valley Forge is synonymous with such a test of character.

The year of warfare following the crossing of the Delaware was another disastrous one for George Washington. The British out-fought and out-maneuvered him to capture Philadelphia where the nation's capital had been.

The only bright spot for the United States that year was an American victory at Saratoga in New York State. A large number of British troops surrendered to the Americans at Saratoga after a bungled attempt to divide the colonies in two by conquering the territory between Canada and New York City.

The victory at Saratoga in October, 1777, led to France entering the war as an American ally on February 6, 1778. But French (and other European) help was still months away as Washington's army took up winter quarters in late 1777 at a place called Valley Forge. (Valley Forge was about 20 miles from Philadelphia, where the victorious British Army was poised to enjoy the winter in comfort.)

While George Washington and his soldiers suffered without proper food and clothing at Valley Forge, jealous officers and foolish politicians blamed him for the loss of New York City in 1776 and of Philadelphia in 1777. They compared Washington's blundering losses with the glorious victory by General Horatio Gates at Saratoga and argued whether to replace Washington as the commander of America's main army. Apparently, such complaining was more entertaining for the politicians than raising the money and supplies needed to help Washington's suffering soldiers.

The suffering at Valley Forge is legendary. Cold. Hunger. Desertions. Blood in the snow from frozen feet.

By the end of the winter, few faithful soldiers remained at Valley Forge. Washington's force had dwindled to about 6,000 half-frozen, half-starving fugitives from the British Army.

By contrast, the British had about 20,000 soldiers—more than three times the number of American soldiers at Valley Forge. Furthermore, the British soldiers were well-fed and well-clothed—much better able to withstand the rigors of a winter campaign than the tattered American soldiers.

Yet the British did not attack. Why?

Once again, British over-confidence played a part. Why fight the Americans in the winter when they could be defeated just as easily in the spring?

Worse yet, the British commander, General Sir William Howe, was enraptured by the charms of his mistress in Philadelphia. He refused to leave the pleasures of her bed for the hazards of war.

And so, like the Roman Empire in its decline and fall, the moral failings of the nation led to military and political failures. (The first volume of Gibbons' classic history, *The Decline and Fall of the Roman Empire*, had just been published the year before this, in 1776.)

A Comment on Modern Revisionism

To be sure, George Washington was not perfect. No one is, except Jesus Christ. We will always be disappointed if we worship anyone other than Jesus Christ[2]—even the Founding Fathers of America. They had their vices and they had their slaves.

But I was dismayed and angered when my daughter, Sarah, told me how her high school history classes intentionally ridicule and denigrate George Washington and other great Americans. Indeed, one reason that I wanted to write this book was to rebuke and refute such flawed history.

For example, in order to cast ridicule on George Washington, Sarah's teacher told the class that George Washington swore frequently and colorfully. I was furious (but I didn't swear).

Instead, I told Sarah that Washington had every right to swear at Valley Forge. His freezing troops were starving and Congress wouldn't supply them with adequate food and clothing.

I also told Sarah that the fact that great people such as George Washington had flaws should not make us think less of them. Instead, we should admire them even more because, despite their many flaws, their many handicaps, and their many weaknesses, they achieved great things. Furthermore, we should be inspired to realize that each of us can also achieve great things despite our many flaws, our many handicaps, and our many weaknesses.

Then I asked how her teacher could *dare* to criticize George Washington. Washington and the other Founding Fathers had risked their lives by rebelling against England—the only "Super Power" of their time. If they'd lost the war, they would surely have been hung.

Moreover, even if the Founding Fathers weren't killed, they could become poor. Mount Vernon stood proudly and vulnerably on the banks of the Potomac, where the British could have burned and sacked it (fortunately, they never did).

Yet this teacher who dared to ridicule and belittle George Washington and the rest of the Founding Fathers would insist that he couldn't be expected to teach children unless his job is protected by tenure. He wouldn't want "political trouble" caused by an unhappy parent to cost him his job—much less his life!

It is just as true that a cup is half full as that it is half empty. And it is far better to look for the ways that the Founding Fathers' lives can inspire and guide us today (the ways that the cup of their lives was full) than to look for ways that the Founding Fathers failed to be perfect (the ways that the cup of their lives was empty).

All of us—except Jesus Christ—have sinned and fallen short of the glory of God. Therefore, rather than trying to paint people as "all good" or "all bad," it is better to see their lives as flawed arrows—or, to use a modern example, to see their lives as "spacecraft to Mars that are a tiny bit off course."

If we try to categorize people as "all good" or "all bad," we will constantly be stupefied that "good people," "good families," "good businesses," "good nations," and "good churches," can sometimes do bad things while "bad people," "bad families," "bad businesses," "bad nations," and "bad churches," can sometimes do good things.

But if we realize that sometimes a "good arrow" *misses* the mark and that sometimes a "bad arrow" *hits* the mark, we will not be so likely to overlook the *bad* that is done by "good people," "good families," "good businesses," "good nations," and "good churches." Nor will we be as likely to overlook the *good* that is done by people, families, businesses, nations, and churches that we perceive as "bad."

We will not waste time feeding our prejudices about who is good or bad. Instead, we will spend our time *profitably*—learning good things that we should do and bad things that we should not do, and living accordingly. We will value each person's life as *good* because we are all created in the image of God. But we will also recognize that each person, apart from Jesus Christ, is flawed and that each of us sins and falls short of the glory of God in significant ways.

Therefore, every organization of humans—*every* family, business, nation and church—is flawed . . . because the people in that family, business, nation and church are flawed. And every organization of humans—*every* family, business, nation and church—falls short of the glory of God.

Even a small error in the course of a spacecraft to Mars can cause it to miss the mark—as was shown recently when one such spacecraft burned up in Mars' atmosphere because NASA mistakenly measured its position in miles instead of in kilometers.[3] Similarly, even a small error in the direction of our lives can ruin many good things that we accomplish. To keep the *spacecraft of our life* on course, we need a perfect directional beacon that guides and corrects us as we move forward each day. That perfect beacon is the Word of God.

The Word of God is *incarnate* as Jesus Christ. And the Word of God is *written* in the Bible. So, in looking at the lives of other people, including the Founding Fathers, we can use the beacon of God's truth to know which aspects of their lives to admire *objectively* rather than *subjectively*.

We know that we should admire only those aspects of others' lives that brought them and their world closer to the Word of God Incarnate (Jesus Christ) and closer to the Word of God Testate (the written Word, *The Holy Bible*).

One such virtue that we learn from the humiliation and suffering of George Washington and his troops at Valley Forge (and from the humiliation and suffering of Jesus on the Cross) is that we must never give in—no matter how much we suffer. We must never give in when we are helping other people by exercising the courage to forge a brighter future for all.

YORKTOWN

It was good that Washington and his soldiers learned fortitude at Valley Forge because the war dragged on for more than three years after this. Throughout, George Washington and his soldiers never had an easy time of it.

To be sure, things were never again *as bad* as at Valley Forge, but the struggle for American independence was hard-fought and prolonged. Eventually, help from European enemies of Britain turned the tide.

Some of this help came from people who shared the ideals of America. For example, Baron von Steuben came from Germany to train the Americans in essential military skills such as marching, loading weapons, and maneuvering on a battlefield.

But the most famous of these European idealists came from France: General Marquis de Lafayette. His enthusiasm and skill made him a key leader of the American Revolution. Indeed, he played a central role in the military campaign of 1781 that ended with the British General Cornwallis and his army being trapped at Yorktown.

Yorktown was a port city on the coast of southern Virginia. It was here that a combined force of French and American troops won the decisive battle of the revolution. Because, in addition to idealists such as Lafayette, the French monarchy under Louis XVI (who would be guillotined a decade later during the French Revolution) sent money, troops, and fleets to fight France's traditional foe: Britain.

Despite significant help from the French, George Washington remained the indispensable man-of-the-hour.[1] No one else could have held the impoverished American army together during years of fruitless war and frustrating stalemate. No one else (but the leader who crossed the Delaware) would have gambled the outcome of the six-year war on one bold, final offensive.

When Lafayette and the American forces fighting with him trapped Cornwallis at Yorktown, Washington was camped outside of New York City. A French army was a short distance away. Yorktown was hundreds of miles to the south. Dirt roads and river crossings lay between.

Nevertheless, Washington and the French did not hesitate. They pretended to be preparing an assault against the British in New York City. But, in fact, the American and French armies marched southward as fast as their legs could carry them. Meanwhile, a French fleet arrived off the coast of Yorktown to blockade the British army that was now trapped there.

The rest is history. The Americans and French besieged Yorktown. Before British reinforcements could arrive by sea from New York City, Cornwallis surrendered. And in London, when the Prime Minister heard the news of the surrender, he lamented, "Oh, God, it is all over!"

The war was over. But the vision of America was just beginning to unfold.

WASHINGTON SENDS THE ARMY HOME

It is an unfortunate truth that most violent revolutions end in tyranny, leading to even more violence. For example, after Cromwell won the English Civil War and set about to establish the power of Parliament and the rights of Englishmen, he executed the king, ruled without Parliament, and led a brutal military campaign against Ireland. In similar fashion, the French Revolution for "Liberty, Equality and Fraternity" led to the execution of the king, the terror of the guillotine, and the imperialist wars of the self-styled "Emperor Napoleon."

Fortunately for America, George Washington was neither a Cromwell nor a Napoleon. Instead, Washington was guided by the example of Cincinnatus, a legendary Roman warrior from the heroic, virtuous days of the Roman Republic—centuries before the tyranny and immorality of the Roman Emperors that led to the decline and fall of the Roman Empire. After saving his nation, Cincinnatus did not make himself into a king, but returned to his farm.[1] Guided by similar personal integrity, after saving America from British tyranny, Washington did not declare himself a king, but returned to his Virginia plantation, Mount Vernon.

Still, danger to American democracy was the greatest in 1783. The peace treaty with Britain had been negotiated and hostilities had ceased. Now the army was free to pursue its complaints against Congress about lack of pay and supplies. Rather than disband, why shouldn't the army march on Congress and demand "justice" at the point of the bayonet?

Only the wisdom and virtue of one man, George Washington, stopped such folly.[2] Because he "never gave in, never gave in, never, never, never, never, except to convictions of honor and good sense"—such as his own personal conviction that he should not become a king or a dictator.

At a mass meeting with his officers on March fifteenth, 1783, Washington desperately sought to instill such honor and good sense in the army. Perhaps the date itself, March 15th, reinforced Washington's resolve to support the Congress rather than to support a popular movement among his men and make himself into a king. Why was this date significant?

The Romans had, for centuries, referred to the fifteenth day of the third month of the year as "The Ides of March." And on one infamous Ides of March, in 44 B.C., Julius Caesar failed to heed the traditional warning, "Beware the Ides of March." On that day, he was assassinated on the steps of the Roman Senate—specifically because some Roman Senators feared that his popularity and power were such that he would make himself into a king.

Fortunately, unlike Julius Caesar, George Washington did not want to become king. Instead of exploiting the army's anger in order to increase his own personal power, he urged patience.

"[D]espite the slowness inherent in deliberative bodies," Washington expressed his faith that Congress would act justly in the end. He told the officers, therefore, that they should not "open the floodgates of civil discord, and deluge our rising empire in blood." Instead, said Washington, they should honorably set a glorious example so that all humanity would see America produce "the last stage of perfection to which human nature is capable of attaining."

Such appeals to honor and good sense were not persuasive. The officers remained disgruntled even after Washington ended his prepared remarks. Hoping that a reassuring letter from a congressman would sway them, Washington pulled the letter from his pocket, but then became confused. The officers leaned forward, afraid that Washington—their beloved leader—might be ill.

Actually, the problem was that Washington's eyesight had become so bad that he couldn't read without glasses. He hated to acknowledge such a sign of weakness and old age, but at last, Washington sheepishly extracted his glasses from his pocket. With some embarrassment, he said, "Gentlemen, you will permit me to put on my spectacles, for I have not only grown gray but almost blind in the service of my country."

They wept.

This simple, sincere statement by Washington touched their hearts, reminding them of their love for him and of the immense sacrifices they *all* had made for the cause of liberty. The crisis was over.

Washington stayed with the army until the British evacuated New York City in late November, 1783. He said goodbye to his officers at Fraunces Tavern. Overcome with emotion at this parting from his comrades, Washington was unable to eat. His hand shook and his lip trembled. Tears streamed down the faces of his officers as Washington embraced each man separately.

Tears also flowed when Washington went to Congress to retire from military life. Rather than becoming a king, he wanted to go home.

George Washington arrived at Mount Vernon on Christmas Eve, 1783. As candles flickered in every window, Martha greeted him at the doorway.

And so, as Thomas Jefferson later paid tribute: "The moderation and virtue of a single character probably prevented this Revolution from being closed, as most others have been, by a subversion of that liberty it was intended to establish."

THE CONSTITUTION

Washington not only acted according to his convictions of honor. He also acted according to his convictions of good sense. And his good sense was never more evident than at the Constitutional Convention in 1787.

Washington had the good sense to understand the times and to know what America should do.[1] As early as 1783—a mere two years after the victory at Yorktown—Washington warned in a letter to the state governments that without a vigorous central government "everything must very rapidly tend to anarchy and confusion." Washington's unheeded advice became known as "Washington's Legacy."[2]

Unfortunately, by 1787 Washington's vision of anarchy and confusion was becoming an apparent reality. The six years since the victory at Yorktown had been a rude awakening for those who naively believed that independence from Britain ensured that they would all live happily ever after.[3]

An economic depression engulfed the country. Despairing farmers in Massachusetts rebelled again. However, this time they fought not against the political tyranny of the British but against the economic tyranny of the debt collector. The rebellion, called Shay's Rebellion, was eventually defeated.

Nevertheless, the fear of more such rebellions spurred people like George Washington into action. These Founding Fathers were determined to establish a strong national government that would ensure a strong economy.

The Founding Fathers also knew that they must have a national ruler who could match the strength and guile of the kings who at that time ruled the world. By 1787, the nation's military and diplomatic weakness had become as depressing as the nation's economic weakness.

For example, the British had not complied with many key provisions of the peace treaty that ended the Revolutionary War. Such humiliations needed to be confronted and put to an end. And only the military strength of a strong national government, together with the diplomatic strength of a strong national leader, could end them.

This sense of crisis encouraged the men gathering in Philadelphia for the Constitutional Convention in 1787 to act boldly. Washington knew that they must cross the "political Delaware" and establish a new, strong central government.

The Constitutional Convention had been called merely to amend the existing governmental framework of the Articles of Confederation. But Washington and the other Founding Fathers thought it best to scrap the Articles of Confederation completely and start over. They set about drafting a constitution that could provide the strong national government needed for the struggling, floundering infant nation.[4]

From their experiences with colonial legislatures, royal governors, and an overbearing central government in distant London, Washington and his fellow leaders knew that strong government could easily be perverted into tyranny. From the political theorists who studied British and French government, the Founding Fathers believed that they could prevent such tyranny by dividing the government's functions between separate legislative, executive, and judicial branches that would check and balance each other's excesses and mistakes.

This good sense, based on experience, faith, and scholarly theory, served the nation well. And throughout the Constitutional Convention Washington was a key dispenser of sensible ideas. Washington was the presiding officer of the sessions, and therefore avoided commenting publicly on issues. But he worked tirelessly behind the scenes at lavish parties and informal tavern meetings to wed experience and theory into workable compromises for all.

At Valley Forge and throughout years of frustrating failures during the Revolutionary War, George Washington followed Churchill's maxim by never giving in. At the Constitutional Convention, he proved his greatness by knowing *when* to give in to convictions of good sense.

Washington knew that, with so many strong leaders expressing differing opinions and models of ideal government, compromise was the only way to establish the future greatness of America. He had the foresight to see, also, that compromise was the only way that convictions of honor and good sense could overcome divisions that sprang from selfishness and folly.

Again and again, Washington found workable compromises that enabled the Constitution to be crafted with wisdom, strength, and durability. The most famous of these compromises has become known as the "Great Compromise" between the large states and the small states. In the Articles of Confederation, each state had one vote in Congress. The small states were happy with this arrangement. Large states complained that their larger populations deserved larger representation in Congress. The Great Compromise was that in the Senate each State would have equal voting power (two Senators per state), but that in the House of Representatives each State would have voting power based on its population.

The most infamous of these compromises were the compromises with slavery and racism. Native Americans were not counted as people unless they had been conquered and were being taxed. Slaves were counted as three fifths of a person. Runaway slaves were required to be returned to their masters. The slave trade could not be abolished for at least twenty years.

These dishonorable compromises would bring great evil upon America. However, two factors should lessen our condemnation of the Founding Fathers for these ill-fated compromises with evil.

First, even Moses had to make compromises with evil. When Jesus said that divorce is bad, his enemies argued that divorce must be good because Moses had permitted it. But Jesus explained that Moses had only permitted divorce because of the hardness of people's hearts (Matthew 19:3–10).

Second, as Abraham Lincoln argued when he explained his views on slavery, the Founding Fathers believed they had set slavery on the road to extinction.[5] They were too ashamed of slavery even to use the word in the Constitution. Instead, the Constitution referred euphemistically to persons "held to service or labour." Furthermore, they fully expected that the slave trade would be abolished once the twenty years of protection granted to it by the Constitution had ended. To appease motivated factions, they allowed for the temporary compromise of their convictions.

A Personal Illustration

My way of approaching such compromises with evil because people's hearts are hard is to compare them with a trip we took by car to Walt Disney World from our home near Rochester, New York. Early in our journey, we were happy when we'd gone far enough to reach Pennsylvania. We knew that this was not our ultimate destination, but contented ourselves with the progress we'd made, confident that we were moving in the right direction and would eventually reach our mark.

Similarly, when the Founding Fathers were just beginning to point humanity toward the road to freedom, they should be commended for their first steps toward protecting all people's rights to life, liberty, and the pursuit of happiness. And we should be merciful in forgiving their blindness to the ways in which they denied such rights to women, blacks, and Native Americans. At least the Founding Fathers were driving their car in the right direction!

Returning to our vacation, it's clear that once we'd driven as far toward Walt Disney World as Virginia, it would have been foolish to turn the car around and start driving back toward Pennsylvania. Similarly, just because someone in the past compromised with evil does not mean that we should make the same shortsighted mistake. Instead, we should drive as fast as we can toward a world that is good and *away* from a world that is evil.

Not only should we do this because it is right, but because compromises with evil will end in God's judgment and wrath–just as America's compromises with the evils of racism and slavery led to horrifying judgment and the wrath of God on America. Lincoln stated that the horrors of the Civil War were divine judgment for the human suffering caused by this crucial error.

By this standard—judging people not by whether they have ever compromised with evil, but by whether their compromises led humanity *toward* good and *away* from evil—George Washington towers above his contemporaries, and even the other Founding Fathers themselves. Washington was the only Founding Father who set his own slaves free.[6] Not even the author of the Declaration of Independence, Thomas Jefferson, believed strongly enough in the unalienable rights of life, liberty, and the pursuit of happiness for all men to set his slaves free.

Although George Washington owned slaves, he decided before the revolution that it was wrong to break up slave families. His refusal to break up families cost him a great deal of money from selling slaves. Furthermore, when George Washington died, his will provided for the gradual emancipation of his slaves in a way that would give them the training needed to be free in *economic fact* as well as free in *legal theory*.

Washington's efforts at gradual emancipation were not very successful because slavery and racism were so strong in America. But at least Washington *tried* to help his own slaves despite the immense odds against his success in transforming society's viewpoint on slavery at that time.

Washington was willing to "cross the Delaware" of slavery and race because he believed that America must eventually destroy slavery or slavery would destroy America. As he told an English visitor, "I clearly foresee that nothing but the rooting out of slavery can perpetuate the existence of our union by consolidating it in a common bond of principle."[7]

Furthermore, Washington disagreed with the racist preconceptions of people such as Thomas Jefferson that blacks were genetically inferior to whites. For example, in 1774 Washington warned that if Americans submitted to British tyranny, "custom and use shall make us as tame and abject slaves as the blacks we rule over with such arbitrary sway."

By inference, it appears that Washington blamed the "arbitrary sway" of white people over black people for the inferior status of African-Americans. Moreover, Washington believed that white people could also be debased to such a sorry condition if they were subjected to the "arbitrary sway" of other people.[8] It is because of such wisdom and such vision that we can truly say that George Washington was "first in war, first in peace, and first in the hearts of his countrymen."[9]

GEORGE WASHINGTON BECOMES PRESIDENT

Naturally, George Washington also became our first President.

He wanted to enjoy a private life at Mount Vernon. But honor required that he serve the nation as President. Only then could he keep faith with the soldiers who suffered to establish a nation where everyone enjoyed the unalienable rights of life, liberty and the pursuit of happiness.

And naturally, while in office Washington again showed his good sense. For example, he had the good sense to keep America out of the wars that were sparked by the French Revolution and the rise of Napoleon. This was an interesting stance for him to take. *Why?*

If Washington had been guided solely by honor, he would have become an ally of revolutionary France. America would have lost its Revolutionary War without the help of France. Furthermore, a treaty allying the United States with France continued to exist. In addition to such formal ties between the United States and France, there were sentimental ties between American lovers of liberty (such as George Washington, Benjamin Franklin, and Thomas Jefferson) and French lovers of liberty (such as Lafayette). For example, after the French Revolution began with the storming of the Bastille, Lafayette sent Washington the key to the Bastille as a tribute to Washington's role as a leader in the fight for people everywhere to be free.[1]

Nevertheless, Washington refused to embroil the young, struggling United States in the wars of Europe. His good sense told him that infant America needed peace with Europe to grow into a powerful nation. Shielded by the Atlantic, America could thrive without meddling by Europeans.

Washington also had the good sense to back Alexander Hamilton's plans for making America a major commercial and industrial power, instead of backing Thomas Jefferson's vision of a purely agricultural nation. Furthermore, Washington did not foster commerce and industry merely so that America could be a wealthy, powerful nation. Foreseeing that slavery was incompatible with commerce and industry, he was eager to set America on an economic course that would undermine, and eventually replace, the plantation system that fostered it.[2]

Finally, Washington had the good sense to retire after two terms as President of the United States instead of staying in office until he died. By setting this precedent that no one should serve as President for more than eight years, Washington went far to ensure that America would never have a king or any other kind of dictator.

Returning to Mount Vernon for the last few years of his life, Washington could rest easy in the knowledge that he had kept faith with the soldiers who suffered with him during the Revolutionary War. A strong, central government existed to preserve the independence of America as a place where all people enjoyed their unalienable rights of life, liberty, and the pursuit of happiness.

The only blemishes on Washington's record were the compromises that he made regarding race and slavery. In my view, we should forgive his inability to overcome these ingrained evils of his society and the eighteenth-century world. As a noted biographer of the first President concluded: "Had Washington been more audacious [in his efforts to free the slaves], he would undoubtedly have failed to achieve the end of slavery, and he would certainly have made impossible the role he played in the Constitutional Convention and the Presidency."[3]

Washington kept faith with America. But America did not keep faith with African-Americans. One tale from around the time when Washington was President captures the frustration and anger of those African-Americans whose patriotism was betrayed. It took place in Boston, a city that prided itself on being the birthplace of freedom.

In Boston, it was common to harass African-Americans at all times, and especially on holidays. One African-American wrote, "How, at such times, are we shamefully abused, and that to such a degree, that we may truly be said to carry our lives in our hands, and the arrows of death are flying about our heads."

During one such Boston riot, a group of whites attacked a group of African-Americans in front of the home of Colonel Middleton, an African-American veteran of the Revolutionary War. "The old soldier stuck a musket out of his door and threatened to kill any white man who approached."

Fortunately, a white neighbor convinced the whites to disperse. (Perhaps the musket also helped to convince the whites that it was time to go.) The neighbor begged Colonel Middleton to put away his gun.

"Colonel Middleton stood silent for a moment." Perhaps he remembered the suffering he endured to win freedom from tyranny. Perhaps he wondered why he had bothered to risk his life for racists who were hypocritical enough to claim that they believed that each person has the unalienable rights of life, liberty, and the pursuit of happiness. "Then he turned and tottered off, dropping his gun and weeping as he went."[4]

We should all weep with Colonel Middleton. Because we must record with shame that America broke faith with African-Americans, who had hoped that the Declaration of Independence meant what it said—that all people have the unalienable right to life, liberty, and the pursuit of happiness.

THE BILL OF RIGHTS

Years passed. Now that George Washington was no longer alive to ensure that honor and good sense guided America, it appeared that the infant nation might be torn asunder by factions and fears.

John Adams followed Washington as President. He was a Federalist, meaning that he tended to favor the development of commerce and industry in the North and to fear the excesses of the French Revolution.

Thomas Jefferson led the Democrats. They tended to favor farming as a way of life and to embrace the ideals of the French Revolution.

Although the Bill of Rights had been added to the Constitution in 1791, the meaning and effectiveness of this safeguard of Americans' human rights remained uncertain. For example, in order to suppress the newspapers that favored Thomas Jefferson and the Democrats, President Adams and the Federalists enacted restrictions on the Freedom of the Press that would never be tolerated today.

When Thomas Jefferson became President in 1801 (after an election that was so close that it had to be decided in the House of Representatives on the 36th ballot), he had the honor and the good sense to end such restrictions on the Freedom of the Press. In his inaugural address, Jefferson declared his distinctly American faith in the good sense of the people, stating that, "[E]rror of opinion may be tolerated where reason is left free to combat it."

Jefferson also affirmed the American faith in the honor of the people when he said: "Majorities must heed the 'sacred principle that, though the will of the majority is in all cases to prevail, that will, to be rightful, must be reasonable,'" and that, "the minority possess their equal rights, which equal laws must protect, and to violate would be oppression."

The Preamble to the Constitution begins with the words, "We the people." Then it lists a number of noble goals that "we, the people" hoped to achieve by establishing the Constitution, such as: forming a more perfect union, establishing justice, promoting the general welfare, and securing the blessings of liberty to ourselves and our posterity.

"We, the people" can only attain such nobility by vindicating the faith that the Bill of Rights and Thomas Jefferson exhibited in upholding the honor and good sense of "We, the people."

To imagine why this is so, consider again the illustration that we, as a nation, are like a spaceship bound for Mars. If we drift too far off course, our doom is certain. Therefore, "we, the people" must constantly check to see whether our spaceship, America, is drifting off course. When this is determined to be the case, "We, the people" must get our spaceship, America, back on course quickly; otherwise, its drift will cause us to miss the target destination entirely.

The Constitution and the Bill of Rights provide the framework for realizing when America is drifting from her foundational values and for getting us back on course. To keep a community on course, we must utilize the insight of every person in that community. Two heads are generally better than one, and "We, the people" are wiser than "I the narrow-minded."

One way to visualize this truth is to think about those "optical illusion" drawings that seem to contain two different pictures depending on your vantage point. In one such drawing, some people at first see a beautiful woman; other people at first see an old hag. When one points out the difference to the other, the other strains for a moment, then sees the drawing differently. By listening to the viewpoint of the person who differs from you, it's possible to see both the hag and the beautiful woman in the same drawing; i.e., to see reality more clearly.

This psychological phenomenon leads to a realization that underlies many aspects of good government: We need one another. For example, it is better to have impartial juries decide lawsuits while each party has his own lawyer. Each lawyer does everything possible to make their client look like the "beautiful woman" and the other party look like the "old hag." Afterwards, the jury decides who looks more like a "beautiful woman" and who looks more like an "old hag."

The division of powers between the executive, legislative, and judicial branches of government ensures illuminating debates and beneficial competition as each eagerly points out ways that the other branches are acting like "old hags" while *it* is acting like a "beautiful woman."

Similarly, to keep America vibrant and free, it is essential to have more than one political party. Each party alerts the public to ways that America is acting like an "old hag" while inspiring people with their vision of how America can become an even more "beautiful woman."

Freedom of the press is, therefore, essential to keeping America vibrant and free because, in any community, including America, it's easy to see only the picture that you want to see. For example, American slave owners claimed that they were treating their slaves well and that the slaves were lucky to have been brought to a Christian land where they could learn how to get to heaven.

The slave owners are like people who refuse to see anything in the drawing except a beautiful woman. But the slaves saw that this *Gone With the Wind* view of slavery was hypocritical nonsense caused by the racism and economic self-interests of slave owners. The slaves saw the truth—that the beauty of the woman, America, was spoiled by the ugliness of those old hags: racism and slavery.

By protecting freedom of the press, we are protecting the ability of the community to share differing viewpoints so that *we, the people* can come to a better understanding of such truths. By having periodic elections, we enable ourselves to get America back on course towards its noble goals: justice and liberty for ourselves and our posterity. Only then can we protect every person's unalienable right to life, liberty, and the pursuit of happiness.

It is worth noting that the church itself is a community that needs "checks and balances," as well as a "Bill of Rights."

Such "checks and balances" and clear statements of rights (and responsibilities) can take many different forms in Christian communities. For example, in our denomination, the Free Methodist, there are periodic General Conferences to establish church policy. At these General Conferences, power is shared equally between the clergy and the laity, differences are discussed openly, and decisions are made by ballot. Term limits ensure that the chief administrative bishop rotates out of power.

Such "checks and balances" and "Bills of Rights" are essential because they keep the "spaceship" called the church on course toward becoming a community in which Christians help each other overcome the "old hags" of our lives and our world. In this way, our lives and our world will become more and more like the "beautiful woman."

Therefore, Christians are far better off seeking the Kingdom of God by living in faith families as "We, the Church" instead of by living in solitude as "I, the Christian." Indeed, it is a collection of such "families" of faith, hope, and love that comprise the true, balanced, and beautiful "Body of Christ" envisioned by St. Paul (1 Corinthians 12:4–13:13).

THE LOUISIANA PURCHASE

By making the Louisiana Purchase, Thomas Jefferson advanced another noble goal of "We, the People" in establishing the Constitution: to "promote the general welfare." Today, when America is a global superpower, straddling the North American continent "from sea to shining sea," it is hard to remember that America was once merely a narrow strip of settlements stretching along the Atlantic seaboard. If European powers such as England and France had prevented American expansion westward, America would have remained a weak nation instead of growing into a world power.

Therefore, as part of the peace treaty that gave America its independence, the British were reluctant to give America control over what today we would call the Midwest. Indeed, the slowness of the British to hand over their forts in the Midwest helped to convince Americans to form a strong, central government.[1]

Even after the British army had withdrawn and American settlers were flocking into the Midwest, perceptive people realized that American ownership was not the same as American control, especially in those distant days when there were no canals, no railroads, and no interstate highways to link the Midwest with the East Coast.[2]

Instead of going to the East Coast, most agricultural products of the Midwest were shipped down the Ohio River until they reached the mighty Mississippi. At New Orleans (near the mouth of the Mississippi River), they were loaded on ships that traveled the world. As a young man, Abraham Lincoln made such trips down the Mississippi to New Orleans a few decades after the Louisiana Purchase.[3]

Clearly, control of the Mississippi River and New Orleans was of immense strategic importance to early Americans. As President Jefferson wrote to his envoy in Paris: "There is on the globe one single spot the possessor of which is our natural and habitual enemy. It is New Orleans, through which the produce of three eighths of our territory must pass to market."[4]

Napoleon and Jefferson both foresaw that the Louisiana Purchase would be the key step in transforming America from a weak nation into a major power. Indeed, one reason that Napoleon sold so much territory to America was in order to create a strong rival to English pretensions around the world. He declared, "The sale assures forever the power of the United States, and I have given England a rival who, sooner or later, will humble her pride."[5]

Besides all of this Napoleonic bluster, there were some stark realities that encouraged Napoleon's decision. Napoleon's treasury was depleted. He needed the $15 million from the Louisiana Purchase to finance his wars in Europe.[6]

Furthermore, Napoleon knew that no one—not even the French under as great a military genius as himself—could win a war in distant America against the combined naval power and armies of England and America. Indeed, Napoleon was stunned to learn that he could not even maintain control of Haiti against a local army of former slaves.[7]

Haitian slaves had won their freedom in 1791 after a bloody uprising–inspired by the same love of "liberty, equality, and fraternity" that was convulsing Paris during the days before the French Revolution. News of Haitian slaves burning plantations and murdering slave owners did *not* inspire American slave owners with hope that some day they could share *liberty, equality, and fraternity* with their former slaves. On the contrary, memories of Haiti's burning plantations and murdered slave owners inspired *nightmares* in the South about potential slave uprisings.

The South lived in perpetual terror that someday the American slaves would rise up and take revenge for generations of whippings and lynchings. The South feared that American slaves would punish them in accordance with the justice of the Old Testament: an eye for an eye, a tooth for a tooth, and a life for a life.

In Haiti, the slave uprising led to a stable government under the brilliant leadership of a former slave, Toussant L'Ouverture. Nevertheless, Haiti remained under the theoretical control of France.

Eventually, Napoleon sent an army to re-assert French control of the island. By trickery, Toussant L'Ouverture was arrested and imprisoned. He died in April, 1803. Nevertheless, the former slaves would not be intimidated. They won a war against Napoleon in which their best weapons were the tropical diseases that killed Europeans so easily.

Napoleon had had enough. His problems in Europe were far more important than his problems with the pesky former slaves of Haiti. In 1803, Napoleon sold New Orleans and the territory drained by the Mississippi River to America—the central third of the continental United States as it exists today.

Jefferson was eager to purchase this territory for a far more important reason than merely to make America a *powerful* nation. He believed that the vast territories of the Louisiana Purchase would keep America a *good* nation: an Empire of Liberty.[8]

Jefferson believed that democracy could flourish best in a nation of farmers. For example, he wrote that "[t]hose who labor in the earth are the chosen people of God, if ever he had a chosen people. Such tillers of the soil are God's 'peculiar deposit for substantial and genuine virtue.'"[9]

Jefferson understood that a nation of farmers achieved a number of social goals that we strive to achieve today in a nation with almost no farmers. On a family-sized farm, everyone has a job. Families live together, work together, and stay together. Children are nurtured and educated. Old people are valued for their wisdom and are cared for in their frailties.[10]

By making the Louisiana Purchase, Jefferson believed that he was obtaining sufficient farmland to sustain this vision of America for centuries to come. To be sure, Jefferson's vision of America was flawed. The plantations in his "Empire of Liberty" used slave labor. Plenty of virtuous people live in cities and suburbs. And nowadays, only a few people in America live on family-sized farms.

Nevertheless, the best part of Jefferson's vision of America continues to inspire us. We still believe that:

- In America, people should have jobs.
- In America, families should live together, work together, and stay together.
- In America, children should be nurtured and educated.
- In America, old people should be valued for their wisdom and should be cared for in their frailties.
- In America, people should seek out new ideas and new opportunities—new "frontiers"—boldly going where no one has gone before.

• And in America, people should live virtuously, turning America into an Empire of Liberty.

The Lewis And Clark Expedition

Another way to "promote the general welfare" is to boldly go where no one has gone before. Columbus showed such boldness. So did Lewis and Clark.

Columbus crossed an unknown ocean. Lewis and Clark crossed an unknown "ocean" of land—the American West. One reason for the Lewis and Clark expedition was political. President Jefferson wanted to solidify American claims to the central and western portions of the North American continent by having Americans explore them. He was fearful that, otherwise, the British might push down from Canada and lay claim to these territories.

But Jefferson had a far more altruistic motive as well. He loved to seek out new lands and make new discoveries for their own sake. It is apparent from reading Jefferson's *Notes on the State of Virginia* (an encyclopedic collection of data that Jefferson gathered about his beloved home state of Virginia) that Jefferson loved to acquire knowledge. In this passion, he was a true child of The Enlightenment.

Naturally, Jefferson jumped at the chance to promote both the national interest and the advancement of human knowledge by sending Lewis and Clark on their now-famous expedition up the Missouri River and across the Rocky Mountains to the Pacific Coast. The most immediate impact of the expedition was on American knowledge of scientific facts. For example, Americans learned that the "purple mountains majesty" out West dwarfed the gentler slopes of the Blue Ridge Mountains in the East.[1]

Americans also learned that vast numbers of buffalo populated fertile plains beneath spacious skies. There was, apparently, a whole new world of things to discover in the vast territories that lay just westward. Therefore, to gain new knowledge in their heads, Americans should boldly go where no one has gone before!

A longer term impact of the expedition was on American understanding of both Native Americans and women. Reflecting two centuries later on the experiences of Lewis and Clark, Americans realized that without the help of Sacagewea, a Native American woman, America's best woodsmen would not have been able to survive. Americans also realized that without the help of a woman, *the same Sacagewea,* her best explorers would have lost their way.

In the long run, what Americans realized about the importance of Native Americans and of women was even more important than what Americans learned about the height of the mountains and the numbers of animals. Therefore, to gain new knowledge in their hearts, Americans should boldly go where no one has gone before!

As Americans meditated two centuries later on the beauty and majesty of the pristine lands that Lewis and Clark had traversed, they fell in love with the mighty mountains and the spacious skies, soaring eagles, and plunging waterfalls. Finally, Americans began working as hard at saving nature (by establishing national parks and protecting wildlife) as Americans used to work at making money, cutting trees, and butchering animals. Therefore, to gain new wisdom in their souls, Americans should boldly go where no one has gone before!

CHAPTER 3

The Last, Best Hope
of Humanity

The Cotton Gin and the Erie Canal

A s Americans, we must not only go boldly to *places* where we have never gone before. To fulfill our vision, we must boldly make *inventions* and construct *marvels* that have never existed before. Since the founding of this country, innovation and creativity—driven by compelling need—have sparked the discovery and development of a myriad of labor-saving and business-expanding ideas.

One such invention was the first cotton gin, built in 1793. By making the processing of cotton much faster, the cotton gin made cotton the material of choice for clothing. As demand for cotton grew, the South grew prosperous along with it.[1]

One such marvel was the Erie Canal, begun in 1817.[2] Western New York state was mostly wilderness before the Erie Canal was built. Scoffers denied that the lengthy man-made waterway could be built. Pessimists doubted that the Erie Canal could ever be profitable.

But the Americans with vision were proven right. Not only was the Erie Canal built—it became a revolutionary success! Now grain and other products from the Midwest could travel east, floating down the Great Lakes to Buffalo, then across New York State on the Erie Canal and the Hudson River, to New York City—from whose magnificent harbor ships could carry cargo down the East Coast and across the world.

With the Erie Canal in place, the prosperity of New York City was assured. New cities such as Buffalo and Rochester quickly sprang up. The Midwest and the Northeast were bound together in a new, free flowing trade and social intercourse.

Largely for this reason, the South took a different path than the Northeast and the Midwest. The South became more and more dependent on cotton, plantations, and slave labor. The Northeast became more and more dependent on commerce and manufacturing. The Midwest followed the path being forged by the Northeast: family-sized farms, vibrant commerce, and growing industries.

Much pain and suffering were to come from the economic, political, ideological, and religious divisions that arose among the distinct geographical sections of America. As early as 1820, Thomas Jefferson foresaw the disastrous consequences of such divisions. The Missouri Compromise—a law admitting a new slave state, Missouri, and a new free state, Maine, and providing that slavery was "forever prohibited" in national territories north of Missouri's latitude—had just been forged.

It was also understood that a new slave-*free* state could not enter the Union unless a new slave-*owning* state entered the Union at the same time. Otherwise, the slave states would be in a minority in the United States Senate. (They were already in a minority in the House of Representatives.)

Commenting on the Missouri Compromise, Jefferson wrote that "this momentous question, like a fireball in the night awakened and filled me with terror. I considered it the knell of the Union."[3]

Tragically, events over the next fifty years were to justify Jefferson's terror at the widening gap between free states and slave states. The Union was preserved only after the suffering and massive bloodshed of the Civil War.

Still, Jefferson's optimism about the future soon returned. A year after writing that he had heard the death knell of the Union, Jefferson wrote:

> And even should the cloud of barbarism and despotism again obscure the science and libraries of Europe, [America] remains to preserve and restore light and liberty to them. In short, the flames kindled on the 4th of July, 1776, have spread over too much of the globe to be extinguished by the feeble engines of despotism; on the contrary, they will consume these engines and all who work them.[4]

Events over the next two hundred years were to justify Jefferson's optimism. When Europe fell under the Nazi cloud of barbarism and despotism, America remained free to preserve and restore light and liberty to Europe, fulfilling Abraham Lincoln's prophecy that America was "the last, best hope of earth"[5]—the last best hope of humanity.

And when the Soviet Union erected an Iron Curtain of barbarism and despotism across the heart of Europe, the flames kindled on the 4th of July, 1776, won the Cold War, extinguishing the feeble engines of despotism and consuming all who worked them.

FREDERICK DOUGLASS AND HARRIETT BEECHER STOWE

In Ancient Israel, God called Isaiah to warn the nation that they were "ever hearing, but never understanding" and "ever seeing, but never perceiving." If the ancient Israelites were ever to be healed from their iniquities, Isaiah told them, they must learn to see with their eyes, hear with their ears, and understand with their hearts (Isaiah 6:9–10).

George Washington faced similar frustrations as a leader. After the revolution, the nation was sinking into chaos and depression because there was not a strong national government. Why didn't Americans perceive the danger and take action?

Washington explained that "the people" can only be "brought slowly into measures of public utility." People "must *feel* before they will *see*."[1]

When it came to slavery, it was as if Americans had eyes, but did not see, and ears, but did not hear. Frederick Douglass and Harriett Beecher Stowe changed all that. By enabling people to *feel* the horrors of slavery, they enabled people to *see* that slavery must be abolished.

Frederick Douglass spent more than twenty years of his life as a slave. He escaped bondage, and within a few years became one of the most spellbinding orators for the Abolitionist Cause.

In 1845, he published a short book titled *Narrative of the Life of Frederick Douglass: An American Slave.*[2] With touching simplicity, Frederick Douglass described what it was like to be a slave. Through his eyes, Americans could see the beatings, hear the weeping, and understand the cruelty of slavery.

Americans could also see that people whose ancestors came from Africa loved freedom as much as people whose ancestors came from England. Frederick Douglass said that even as a child he yearned to be free: "From my earliest recollection, I date the entertainment of a deep conviction that slavery would not always be able to hold me within its foul embrace."[3] He related that, by the time he was about 12 years old, "the thought of being *a slave for life* began to bear heavily upon my heart."[4]

His thirst for freedom turned into a thirst for education. He learned the first steps of reading from a kind mistress who was not used to the ways of slavery. When her husband found out what she was doing, he rebuked her. He warned her that if you teach a slave to read "there would be no keeping him. It would forever unfit him to be a slave."[5]

As Frederick Douglass remembered years later: "These words sank deep into my heart . . . and called into existence an entirely new train of thought." He now understood "the white man's power to enslave the black man."[6] *The whites kept the blacks uneducated!* Therefore, as a child, Frederick Douglass "set out with high hope, and a fixed purpose, at whatever cost of trouble, to learn how to read."[7]

His struggles to learn to read and write far exceeded the oft-described struggles of Abraham Lincoln. Growing up at roughly the same time, Abraham Lincoln's problem was that there weren't many books to read on the frontier. So we inspire school children with tales about how young Abe walked miles to borrow books to read beneath the flickering flame of the fireplace.

In contrast, it was *illegal* for Frederick Douglass to learn to read or write. The slave-owners, including Frederick Douglass's master, well knew that they could only keep the blacks down if they kept the blacks uneducated.

Nevertheless, Frederick Douglass persevered. He learned by using the discarded homework of his master's son. He tricked the neighborhood children into revealing how to write. He snuck around reading everything he could lay his hands on.

Despite his many disadvantages, Frederick Douglass became a great writer, as well as a dynamic orator. He settled in Rochester, New York, only a few miles from where my own family now lives. In 1847, he started publishing his newspaper, the *North Star*. He rose to "the forefront of the abolitionist ranks" and continued to stand "on the watchtower of American freedom, championing the cause of all oppressed men and women" until his death in 1895.[8]

Nevertheless, despite the efforts of Frederick Douglass and many others, only a small, despised minority of Americans were abolitionists before the Civil War. Most northerners viewed slavery as a necessary evil. And southerners praised the "peculiar institution" of American slavery as the best way of life for the supposedly lazy, stupid, inferior black race.

Frederick Douglass denounced such spiritual blindness and deafness in a speech in Rochester, New York on July 5, 1852, that he titled: "What to the Slave Is the Fourth of July?"[9] He spoke with "a sad sense of the disparity between us" because "[t]he blessings in which you this day rejoice, are not enjoyed in common."

Douglass explained to his white listeners: "This Fourth of July is *yours*, not *mine*." Over the tumultuous joy of whites at their

Fourth of July celebrations, he heard "the mournful wail of millions" with "heavy and grievous" chains. He mourned for "those bleeding children of sorrow."

The "hideous and revolting" conduct of the nation meant that "America is false to the past, false to the present, and solemnly binds herself to be false to the future." Therefore, "[s]tanding with God and the crushed and bleeding slave" and "in the name of humanity which is outraged, in the name of liberty which is fettered, in the name of the constitution and the Bible, which are disregarded and trampled upon," Douglass said that he would "dare to call in question and to denounce . . . everything that serves to perpetuate slavery—the great sin and shame of America!"

Douglass refused to waste his time disputing whether slavery was wrong. He asked how it *cannot* be wrong:

> to make men brutes, to rob them of their liberty, to work them without wages, to keep them ignorant . . ., to beat them with sticks, to flay their flesh with the lash, to load their limbs with irons, to hunt them with dogs, to sell them at auction, to sunder their families, to knock out their teeth, to burn their flesh, to starve them into obedience and submission to their masters?

Douglass told his audience that:

> [t]he feeling of the nation must be quickened; the conscience of the nation must be roused; the propriety of the nation must be startled; the hypocrisy of the nation must be exposed; and its crimes against God and man must be proclaimed and denounced. Otherwise, the celebration of the Fourth of July is a sham; your boasted liberty, an unholy license; your national greatness, swelling vanity; your sounds of rejoicing are empty and heartless; your denunciations of tyrants, brass-fronted impudence; your shouts of liberty and equality, hollow mockery; your prayers and hymns, your sermons and thanksgivings, with all your religious parade and solemnity, are to [a slave] mere bombast, fraud, deception, impiety, and hypocrisy.

To Douglass, all such celebrations of liberty in America were "a thin veil to cover up crimes which would disgrace a nation of savages." The sad Truth was that "[t]here is not a nation on the earth guilty of practices more shocking and bloody, than are the people of these United States, at this very hour." Douglass concluded his speech with the horrifying thought that "for revolting barbarity and shameless hypocrisy, America reigns without a rival."

Fortunately, in that very same year of 1852, Harriett Beecher Stowe published *Uncle Tom's Cabin*. The impact of her book was so great that, when Abraham Lincoln met Harriett Beecher Stowe a decade later in 1862, he said, "So this is the little lady who made this big war?"

Harriett Beecher Stowe's fictional account of Uncle Tom's life as a Christian slave enabled whites (at least in the North) to see with their eyes, hear with their ears, and understand with their hearts. She enabled Americans to see the tears of mothers and their children who were separated forever because they were sold to different masters.

She enabled Americans to hear the moans of Uncle Tom when he became a martyr (Uncle Tom was whipped to death when he refused to betray the whereabouts of two female slaves who had run away rather than continue to be sex toys.)

She enabled Americans to understand that they were hypocrites to talk about loving liberty while they were enslaving others. She enabled Christians to understand that they must stop permitting other good Christians such as Uncle Tom to be persecuted as slaves.

Few people read *Uncle Tom's Cabin* anymore. It is written in a syrupy style that dropped out of fashion long ago. Modern readers are uneasy about its many racist stereotypes. Furthermore, modern readers squirm as Uncle Tom meekly submits to outrage after outrage while singing hymns and quoting Bible verses. Nowadays, no one wants to be known as an "Uncle Tom."

Nevertheless, when *Uncle Tom's Cabin* was first published, it was fantastically successful. In the South, people denounced the book as slanderous. But across the North, people became more and more outraged by slavery, and more and more determined to end this blight upon America.

God's Truth was marching on. Americans could see the evils of slavery with their eyes, hear the evils of slavery with their ears, and understand the evils of slavery with their hearts.

SOJOURNER TRUTH AND HARRIETT TUBMAN

Frederick Douglass warned Americans that they must earn their liberty through struggle. "The whole history of the progress of human liberty," he said, "shows that all concessions yet made to her august claims, have been born of earnest struggle. . . . If there is no struggle there is no progress."[1]

He heaped scorn on those who naively hoped that liberty for the slaves could be won without struggle. He said, "Those who profess to favor freedom and yet deprecate agitation, are men who want crops without plowing up the ground, they want rain without thunder and lightning. They want the ocean without the awful roar of its many waters."

This struggle would take many forms. It "may be a moral one, or it may be a physical one, and it may be both moral and physical, but it must be a struggle."

Such struggles are necessary because "[p]ower concedes nothing without a demand. It never did and it never will." Douglass's words began to light a spark in the hearts of future leaders.

Two leaders of the struggle to free the slaves were Sojourner Truth and Harriett Tubman.

Sojourner Truth struggled primarily in the moral realm. She traveled the land like an Old Testament prophet, proclaiming the Truth of the Lord. For a biblical "forty years," she preached. Sinners who loved slavery hated her. Saints who hated slavery loved her.

For example, Harriett Beecher Stowe never forgot the sight of this former slave. Stowe described Sojourner Truth as a gaunt, misty-eyed woman wearing a gray dress, a white turban and a sunbonnet, standing calm and erect, like "one of her native palm trees waving alone in the desert." Stowe recalled, "She seemed perfectly self-possessed and at her ease; in fact, there was almost an unconscious superiority in the odd, composed manner in which she looked down on me."[2]

Meanwhile, Harriett Tubman struggled primarily in the physical realm. She escaped from slavery using the Underground Railway at the age of 25. Utterly determined to win her liberty and the liberty of others, she explained:

> I had reasoned this out in my mind; there was one or two things I had a *right* to, liberty or death; if I could not have one, I would have the other; for no man should take me alive; I should fight for my liberty as long as my strength lasted, and when the time come for me to go, the Lord would let them take me.

Amazingly, Harriett Tubman returned to the South again and again to lead others to freedom along the Underground Railway. The rewards for her capture reached $40,000. Nevertheless, she persevered. On her 19 trips to the South, she freed more than 300 slaves.

One abolitionist said, "She deserves to be placed first on the list of American heroines." Another ranked her with Joan of Arc.[3]

Unfortunately, the struggles of Sojourner Truth and Harriett Tubman were not nearly enough to win liberty for the slaves. That struggle—the Civil War—would be the bloodiest in American history. That struggle would not stop until the South lay prostrate and the slaves were free.

Most Americans in the 1850s could not imagine the disaster that awaited them within a few years. But Harriett Beecher Stowe sounded a warning. At the end of *Uncle Tom's Cabin*, she reminded the church that, according to the Bible, Christ "shall break in pieces the oppressor." And she warned Americans that these are "dread words for a nation bearing in her bosom so mighty an injustice."

Nevertheless, Harriett Beecher Stowe did not yet abandon all hope for a peaceful end to slavery. As she put it, "[a] day of grace is yet held out to us."

However, she saw, heard, and understood the evil in America and in the Church. She wrote, "Both North and South have been guilty before God; and the *Christian Church* has a heavy account to answer."

Harriett Beecher Stowe rejected the compromises (such as the Missouri Compromise and the Compromise of 1850) that politicians crafted to save the Union for white people at the expense of black people. She accurately foresaw that the Union could not be saved "by combining together, to protect injustice and cruelty, and making a common capital of sin." The Union could only be saved "by repentance, justice, and mercy."

Therefore, Harriett Beecher Stowe ended *Uncle Tom's Cabin* with a prophecy of doom: if America did not take the path of "repentance, justice, and mercy," there was no doubt that the "injustice and cruelty" in America would bring "the wrath of Almighty God!"

ABRAHAM LINCOLN VERSUS STEPHEN DOUGLAS

In every great novel, the protagonist must prove his greatness by fighting and overcoming a powerful antagonist. In the life of Abraham Lincoln, this antagonist was Stephen Douglas. (Notice that *this* Douglas only used one "s" in his name, in contrast to Frederick Douglass who used two.)

Even in appearance, the two men could not have been more different. Lincoln was tall and ungainly. His voice was "a piercing tenor, which at times became shrill and sharp." His clothes *never* seemed to fit well.[1]

Douglas was a short man, barely reaching the shoulders of Lincoln. Nevertheless, Douglas, with his commanding head and deep baritone voice, became known as The Little Giant "because his [political] power belied his size." He was the epitome of the well-dressed man.[2]

Lincoln "felt embarrassed about his log cabin origins and never liked to talk about them."[3] He once described his early years as, "The short and simple annals of the poor."[4]

Even after his successful legal practice made him a fairly wealthy man, Lincoln continued to have simple tastes. Indeed, to sway voters he deliberately cultivated his image "as a countryman, shrewd and incorruptible."[5]

By contrast, Douglas deliberately cultivated his image as "a commanding figure, a statesman of national reputation." He liked to travel "by special train, splendidly fitted out for comfort and for entertaining." When he addressed crowds, he liked to stand in a handsome blue suit with silver buttons and immaculate linen.[6]

Both men were ambitious. Lincoln's law partner, Billy Herndon, put it this way: Lincoln "was always calculating, and always planning ahead. His ambition was a little engine that knew no rest."[7]

Douglas was, if anything, even more ambitious than Lincoln. But in startling contrast to the setbacks and ill fortune that seemed to haunt Lincoln's life, Douglas quickly became admired and powerful. This must have irked Lincoln more than any other difference between the two men.

For example, when Douglas was elected to the Illinois Legislature at the age of twenty-three, he "instantly assumed leadership of the Democrats" because he "had already mastered the arts of legislative politics."[8] Within a few years, Douglas became a United States Senator. Within a few more years, Douglas became the most powerful man in the Senate.

By comparison to such triumphs, Lincoln's mundane political career was a disappointing mediocrity. He served about a decade in the Illinois legislature. Like a typical politician, he passed legislation that helped his supporters' economic interests—such as banks and railroads. And, like a typical politician, he helped his supporters get government jobs.

Lincoln then served one term in Congress, doing nothing noteworthy. Worse yet, he alienated many of the voters back home by criticizing the way that President Polk manipulated events to start a war with Mexico in 1846.

President Polk's war with Mexico ended in a stunning United States victory that forced Mexico to transfer about half of its territory, including California, to the United States. Elated voters and returning veterans did not want their consciences pricked by arguments that the United States was morally wrong for provoking the war. So Lincoln quietly retired from Congress and devoted himself to making money as a successful trial attorney.[9]

Abraham Lincoln also devoted himself to his wife, Mary Todd Lincoln.[10] In her courting days, she had known both Douglas and Lincoln. She "flirted outrageously" with Douglas,[11] but she married Lincoln. Years later, when someone dared to compare her husband unfavorably to Douglas, she shot back: "Mr. Lincoln may not be as handsome a figure . . . but the people are perhaps not aware that his heart is as large as his arms are long."[12]

Although Lincoln no longer ran for public office after his retirement from Congress, he stayed active in politics behind the scene. He campaigned for other people, building IOUs that he hoped might someday enable him to become the United States Senator from Illinois.

In 1852 he made a series of campaign speeches supporting the Whig candidate for President. Discouragement at his many disappointments sapped his old vigor. His speeches fell flat. Lincoln showed his old spark only when he was insulting his despised nemesis, Stephen Douglas, who was campaigning to become the Democratic candidate for President.

Lincoln "sneered" at Douglas's pretensions sarcastically. "The edge to Lincoln's remarks went beyond campaign banter and suggested his disappointment that his old rival Douglas, now the most powerful member of the United States Senate, was 'a giant,' while Lincoln remained one of the 'common mortals.'"[13]

Then the furor over slavery transformed the life of Abraham Lincoln. The moral passion that entered Lincoln's heart turned him from a good speaker into a great orator, from a typical politician into a great statesman.

Jealousy played a role, too. Because the person who sparked this transformation of Abraham Lincoln into a legendary leader was none other than the Little Giant, Stephen Douglas, who led the battle that repealed the Missouri Compromise.

To understand why the North was so alarmed by the repeal of the Missouri Compromise, it is necessary to review some history. As you may remember, during the decades leading up to the Civil War, there were a number of compromises between the North and the South to keep the Union together.

The first of these compromises was the Missouri Compromise in 1820 that prohibited slavery in Federal territories north of Missouri's latitude. It was this compromise that prompted Thomas Jefferson to write: "this momentous question, like a fireball in the night awakened and filled me with terror. I considered it the knell of the Union."

The last great compromise between the North and the South was the Compromise of 1850. This compromise was the crowning achievement of the life and career of Henry Clay, a Senator who was known as the Great Compromiser.

Abraham Lincoln worshipped Henry Clay. They were both members of the Whig Party. And, as we shall see, Abraham Lincoln himself was a Great Compromiser as he tried to avert the Civil War, as he held diverse factions in the Republican party and in the North together during the Civil War, and as he began to reconstruct the Union after the Civil War "with malice toward none and with charity for all."

In making these compromises, the North was confident that slavery would never spread into the free states or the free territories of the North. This principle was established as early as the Northwest Ordinance of 1787.[14] This principle was also the core of the Missouri Compromise in 1820.

Northern complacency about the spread of slavery began to erode when, as part of the Compromise of 1850, the South insisted on tougher Federal measures to return runaway slaves. Under this Federal law, Northerners were forced to enslave people and send them back to the South where they were punished harshly for daring to seek the same freedoms that Americans hypocritically celebrated every Fourth of July.

It was no longer possible to think of slavery as a uniquely Southern problem. Slavery was now becoming a curse on the North as well. Harriett Beecher Stowe published *Uncle Tom's Cabin* in 1852 because she was outraged that the fugitive slave law punished Christians for helping people escape slavery. Indeed, the most famous scene in her book describes how a mother fled slavery in Kentucky by taking her child (who was about to be sold so that she would never see him again) to the free state of Ohio. With the slave traders in hot pursuit, she jumped across treacherous ice in the frozen Ohio River. Even after this heroic feat, this noble mother and her child were not safe from being tracked like animals, kidnapped, and returned to slavery. Ultimately, they had to escape from our so-called "Land of the Free" by going to Canada.

The anger of Northerners at such evil occurring in their midst sometimes boiled over into mob violence. In 1851, a mob in Syracuse, New York, rescued a fugitive slave named Jerry McHenry who had been captured in that Northern state. Mr. McHenry fled to Canada and no one was punished for defying the law.

In 1854, a mob in Boston tried to rescue a fugitive slave named Anthony Burns. They failed, but it took 1100 soldiers to escort Mr. Burns to the ship that carried him back to Virginia. (The story had a happy ending because some Boston citizens purchased Mr. Burns the next year and set him free.)[15]

Therefore, the repeal of the Missouri Compromise in 1854 was the last straw for many Northerners. This blunder by Stephen Douglas stripped away the naive illusion that slavery could exist in the South without threatening freedom in the North. Throughout the Northeast and the Midwest, millions of people from all political parties realized that they could no longer—*must* no longer—ignore slavery. Indeed, many people in the North feared that the South was plotting to spread slavery throughout every territory and state in the Union.

As Lincoln put it, the repeal of the Missouri Compromise "took us by surprise—astounded us . . . We were thunderstruck and stunned."[16]

Northerners could no longer hide their heads in the sand. They were forced to see the evils of slavery, to hear the weeping caused by slavery, and to understand that the existence of slavery for blacks in the South hurt whites in the North, too. Therefore, opposition to Stephen Douglas's repeal of the Missouri Compromise became the central issue in the elections of 1854. There were calls for "an organization of men of whatever politics, of Free Soilers, Whigs, and Democrats, who should bury past animosities, and . . . unite in hurling down the gigantic evil which threatened even their own liberty."[17]

Lincoln remained silent for a number of months, pondering the best role for himself to take. Finally, ignoring the calls to forge a new political party, he decided to remain a faithful Whig by campaigning in support of the local Whig candidate for Congress. He campaigned against "the great wrong and injustice of the repeal of the Missouri Compromise, and the extension of slavery into free territory."[18]

Fired up by the threat to America, Lincoln's speeches became impassioned and inspiring. The climax of the 1854 campaign came when Lincoln spoke at the Illinois State Fair in response to a speech by Douglas the previous day. Douglas sat directly in front of Lincoln during the speech and sometimes bantered with Lincoln as he spoke.

Lincoln spoke to the attentive crowd for three hours. Although he started a bit awkwardly with a voice that was "sharp, shrill, piping and squeaky," the pitch of his voice "became harmonious, melodious, musical" as he warmed to his task.

The intellectual substance of his arguments was not new. Other orators had been denouncing the repeal of the Missouri Compromise for months.

What was new was Lincoln's "tone of moral outrage when he discussed 'the monstrous injustice of slavery.'" Lincoln reviewed how the Founding Fathers had set slavery on the road to extinction because they "hedged and hemmed it in to the narrowest limits of necessity." They were so ashamed of slavery that they did not even use the word "slavery" in the Constitution. Instead, they used euphemisms. In Lincoln's words, the Founding Fathers acted toward slavery "just as an afflicted man hides away a wen or a cancer, which he dares not cut out at once, lest he bleed to death; with the promise, nevertheless, that the cutting may begin at the end of a given time."

In contrast, the repeal of the Missouri Compromise meant that America was openly tolerating this monstrous evil of slavery. Therefore, "Lincoln reached a new oratorical height in denouncing Douglas's claim that he was merely acting in the spirit of the Founding Fathers in permitting self-government in the territories."

As Lincoln denounced this heresy, he "quivered with feeling and emotion" and "his feelings once or twice swelled within and came near stifling utterance."

And no wonder. From his earliest years, Lincoln read history books in which the Founding Fathers were portrayed as infallible demigods. As a self-made man who became a successful lawyer despite grinding poverty and little formal education, the bedrock of Lincoln's political faith was that all men are created equal—that all men must have an equal opportunity to succeed as he had succeeded.

Slavery denied such equal opportunity to blacks *directly*, by keeping them from enjoying the fruits of their labor. And slavery was beginning to deny equal opportunity to whites *indirectly*, by making white people compete against slave labor.

Lincoln worried that the spread of slavery would drive wages lower for white workers, making many white people as poor as black slaves. He also had come to realize the worldwide implications of America tolerating slavery. In a eulogy of Henry Clay after his death in 1852, Lincoln echoed Clay's feeling "that the world's best hope depended on the continued Union of these States."

Accordingly, Lincoln warned the crowd at the Illinois State Fair that we are "proclaiming ourselves political hypocrites before the world" because we are "fostering human slavery and proclaiming ourselves, at the same time, the sole friends of human freedom."

Douglas spent two hours rebutting Lincoln's arguments. But the damage to Douglas was done. Abraham Lincoln had found the passion to change from a typical politician into the greatest statesman of his generation.[19]

Therefore, politicians in Illinois increasingly sought Lincoln's support for forming a new political party. This new party drew support from people of both existing political parties—the Democrats and the Whigs—who were opposed to the extension of slavery. They called this new political party the Republican Party.

In 1856, Lincoln attended the convention that organized the Republican Party in Illinois. Now forty-seven years old, he bought his first pair of spectacles while waiting for the convention to begin. The unwitting symbolism was perfect. Because at this convention his stirring speech showed that he saw slavery's evils and the hope of Americans better than anyone else.

As Lincoln's law partner recalled later, "His speech was full of fire and energy and force; it was logic; it was pathos; it was enthusiasm; it was justice, equity, truth and right set ablaze by the divine fires of a soul maddened by the wrong; it was hard, heavy, knotty, gnarly, backed with wrath."[20]

In this speech, Lincoln revealed the passion that would carry both himself and the Union through four bloody years of civil war. He pledged that he was "ready to fuse [politically] with anyone who would unite with him to oppose slave power." And if the South dared to raise "the bugbear [of] disunion," the answer should be that "*the Union must be preserved in the purity of its principles as well as in the integrity of its territorial parts.*"[21]

The legendary orator and U.S. Senator from Massachusetts, Daniel Webster, said much the same thing during a Senate debate over the fate of the Union in 1830. Now, Lincoln quoted Daniel Webster's eloquence to forge the motto of the newly-founded Republican Party: "Liberty *and* Union, now and forever, one and inseparable."[22]

FORT SUMTER

Abraham Lincoln and Stephen Douglas continued to battle each other—steel against steel.

During the campaign for the U.S. Senate in 1858, they engaged in a series of debates that attracted huge crowds and lasted for hours. These events are remembered in history as "The Lincoln/ Douglas Debates."

Douglas won the political battle. He was re-elected to the U.S. Senate. (Since Senators were chosen by the majority party in the state legislature, voters could not make a direct choice between Douglas and Lincoln.)

Yet ultimately, Lincoln won the war. By standing toe-to-toe with Douglas, the most powerful man in the Senate, Lincoln rose to national stature. Furthermore, texts of the debates were printed across the United States, familiarizing people with his views. Lincoln began making speaking tours across the northern states.

In 1860, few people thought that Lincoln was likely to be nominated for President by the Republican Party. Nevertheless, through a combination of shrewd politicking and striking good luck, Lincoln won the Republican nomination.

In fact, the leading candidate for the Republican nomination was Senator James L. Seward of New York State, a widely-known national leader. Nevertheless, Lincoln's views appeared to be more moderate than Seward's. Because of a speech Seward gave in Rochester, New York, in 1858, "Southerners and others" felt that Seward was a dangerous *warmonger.*

In this hotbed of abolitionist sentiment—where the Underground Railroad was crowded with slaves fleeing to Canada and where Frederick Douglass published his newspaper, *North Star,* Seward spoke of an "irrepressible conflict" between the North and the South. Seward also frightened people with his talk of a "higher law" which justified disobedience to Federal laws.[1]

Although Lincoln's views were not much different from Seward's, Lincoln expressed his views more tactfully. Lincoln's prediction that a "house divided" could not remain half slave and half free, but must become *all* one thing or *all* the other, amounted to much the same thing as Seward's prediction of an "irrepressible conflict."[2] But people preferred Lincoln's illustration, based on a proverb of Jesus, to Seward's blunt talk about unavoidable bloodshed.

Similarly, despite Lincoln's protestations to the contrary,[3] there was not much difference between Seward's views about a "higher law" than the Constitution and Lincoln's belief that the Union derived from the Declaration of Independence in 1776 instead of from the Constitution in 1787. "The concept of the Union, older than the Constitution, deriving from the Declaration of Independence with its promise of liberty for all, had become the premise on which all [Lincoln's] other political beliefs rested."[4]

Once again, however, Lincoln's ways of expressing himself were more palatable than Seward's. Seward's talk of a "higher law" than the Constitution sounded revolutionary. Lincoln's praise of the Declaration of Independence sounded patriotic.

Republicans picked Abraham Lincoln as their nominee for President because his moderate views made him more likely to appeal to large numbers of voters across the Northeast and the Midwest.[5] The South, however, did not view Lincoln as a moderate candidate. They viewed him as a dangerous abolitionist and a warmonger.

As hard as it is to believe, Lincoln did not receive even *one* vote in ten Southern states.[6] Indeed, the South had become so alienated from the rest of the country that southern Democrats refused to support the candidate of northern Democrats, Stephen Douglas.

Lincoln crushed Douglas throughout the Northeast and the Midwest, winning the election.[7] The Republicans also took control of the Congress.

The South recoiled in horror. They did not believe that Abraham Lincoln could be trusted to keep his oft-repeated promise that he would not tamper with slavery in states where it already existed—that he only sought to prevent the *spread* of slavery.

Southern leaders were convinced that Republican policies would destroy the South's slave-based economy. And Southern demagogues fanned fears that Republican policies would cause the slaves to revolt—"raping white women and murdering white families."

Maddened by such fears, the South took a foolish course. As has often been noted, if the South had stayed in the Union, they could have prevented the Republicans in Congress from passing legislation that was harmful to Southern interests. Furthermore, the Supreme Court was sympathetic to Southern views that the Constitution protected their right to own slaves.[8] Then, after four years of an ineffectual Lincoln administration, the South probably could have elected a Democratic candidate for President merely by backing the same candidate as Northern Democrats.

Clearly, if the South had not reacted in fear and panic, they would have realized that they "had nothing to fear but fear itself." But it is the nature of sin to deceive us. Fears caused by centuries of mistreatment of African-Americans overwhelmed such rational, common sense ideas as staying in the Union and driving the Republicans from power in coming elections.

Remember that Southern fears of a future without slavery were not merely economic fears. (Although running the South's economy without slaves seemed as impossible to them as running our economy without electricity seems impossible to us.)

Southerners faced a far more fearful prospect. They had enslaved and mistreated African-Americans for over two centuries. If these people were set free, what would stop them from wreaking a terrible vengeance upon whites? The South could not forget the dreadful slaughter of whites when the slaves revolted in Haiti.

As proof of the Republican threat to Southern lives, the South pointed to those Republicans who thought that John Brown was a hero for trying to start a slave revolt. (About a year before Lincoln's election, John Brown and a group of fanatics took hostages and seized weapons stored at Harpers Ferry. Robert E. Lee led the U.S. Marines who ended this terrorist act.)[9]

Aware of Southern passions, some experienced politicians in the North urged Lincoln to calm Southern fears during the months between his election in November, 1860, and his inauguration on March 4, 1861. He rejected their suggestions, siding with most of the leaders of the Republican Party. They thought it was best for

Lincoln to remain silent until he actually took the reins of power in March.

Lincoln (and the Republican leaders who urged him to remain silent) did not take Southern bluster about leaving the Union as seriously as did better-informed Republicans in Congress. Placing his faith in the Southerners who had been his colleagues in Congress during the 1840s, Lincoln believed "that Unionists were in a large majority throughout the South and that, given time for tempers to cool, they would be able to defeat" the movement to leave the Union.[10]

Lincoln vastly underestimated the South's fears and the South's resolve. Fearing the destruction of their economy by Republican economic policies that favored the North and fearing the destruction of their lives by rebellious slaves, Southern states began leaving the Union.

The first to leave was South Carolina on December 20. Six more states left the Union before Lincoln could even take the oath of office. In February, the seceding states united to form the Confederate States of America.[11]

No wonder that, when Abraham Lincoln said farewell to a crowd of well-wishers at the train station in Springfield, he said, "I now leave . . . with a task before me greater than that which rested upon Washington."[12]

What Lincoln did not publicly acknowledge, but what must have weighed on his heart, was the realization that he was the least prepared person ever to become President. He had almost no formal education. He had no administrative experience. He had served a mere two years in Congress. He had held no public office for ten years. He seemed to fail at everything he ever tried.[13]

To buttress his self-confidence in the face of so many flaws and failures, Lincoln relied on a fatalistic trust in Divine Providence that he'd learned as a child. Although Lincoln never joined a church, he read the Bible, *Pilgrim's Progress* and other books that taught Christian morality. Therefore, his speeches were laced with references from the Bible (such as a house being divided against itself). And, he told the well-wishers at the train station in Springfield:

"Without the assistance of that Divine Being, who ever attended [George Washington], I cannot succeed. With that assistance I cannot fail." He asked the people for their prayers and bid them "an affectionate farewell."[14]

In his Inaugural Address, Lincoln did his best to calm the fears of the South. Although he insisted that he would "hold, occupy, and possess property and places belonging to the government" (such as Fort Sumter), he promised that "no bloodshed or violence" was necessary;[15] He ended with this eloquent plea for peace:

> We are not enemies, but friends. We must not be enemies . . . The mystic chords of memory, stretching from every battlefield, and patriot grave, to every living heart and hearthstone, all over this broad land, will yet swell the chorus of the Union, when again touched, as surely they will be, by the better angels of our nature.[16]

Nevertheless, the crisis deepened. The South focused on the parts of his Inaugural Address where Lincoln pledged to reclaim federal property and enforce the tariff. Full of fear and distrust, a Charleston, South Carolina paper labeled gawky Abraham Lincoln as "the Ourang-Outang at the White House" and told its readers that he had sounded "the tocsin of battle." A paper in Richmond, Virginia warned that Lincoln's Inaugural Address inaugurated civil war.[17]

The new President quickly learned that the situation at Fort Sumter was far worse than he had realized. In about six weeks, Fort Sumter would run out of supplies. Furthermore, there was no easy way to resupply Fort Sumter because it lay in the middle of the harbor in Charleston, South Carolina, where Confederate artillery encircled it.[18]

Deeply alarmed, Lincoln and others began looking for a way to defuse the crisis. There was even some support for a constitutional amendment that would forever guarantee the existence of slavery in the South.[19]

No wonder Frederick Douglass despaired.

Again and again in American history, whites in the North and the South had compromised their differences by sacrificing the liberty of blacks. In 1787, at the Constitutional Convention, whites compromised by permitting the slave trade to continue for at least another 20 years.[20] In 1820, whites compromised by permitting the South to add new slave states and by promising the North that slavery (and cheap black labor) wouldn't spread to the North. In 1850, whites compromised by agreeing that the North would increase its efforts to return runaway slaves to their masters in the South.

Now, in 1861, it looked as if whites in the North might compromise to preserve the Union by adopting a constitutional amendment that would guarantee that slavery could exist forever in the South. How would the new president respond?

As a practical politician, Lincoln was willing to compromise any issues except "the extension of slavery into the national territories"—not because Lincoln was worried about the effect of extending slavery on black people—but because Lincoln feared that a compromise on extending slavery into the national territories "would disrupt the party that had elected him."[21]

All of this talk of compromise by whites at the expense of blacks was a far cry from Abraham Lincoln's motto for the Republican Party: "Liberty *and* Union, now and forever, one and inseparable." Therefore, Frederick Douglass attacked Lincoln's timidity. In an editorial, he complained that, "With the single exception of the question of slavery extension, Mr. Lincoln proposes no measure which can bring him into antagonistic collision with the traffickers in human flesh."[22]

Weary with such betrayals of his people, Frederick Douglass lost hope. "Disappointed by Lincoln's Inaugural Address, alarmed by public persecution, he fear[ed] for his people. For the first time in twenty years, he [lost] faith in the American Dream." Wondering whether blacks would be better off fleeing America, Douglass chartered a boat to investigate Haiti as a possible haven.[23]

Then the South made a fatal mistake. Hotheads in South Carolina didn't merely want Fort Sumter to be abandoned because it ran out of food. They wanted to take credit for *forcing* Fort Sumter to surrender.

These shortsighted fools did not see the bloodshed of war. They were too blinded by delusions of glory. These deaf prophets did not hear the weeping that comes from needless death and suffering. They were too deafened by talk of glory. These wicked men did not understand that starting a war would enable Lincoln to do something that he could never have done in peacetime: free the slaves.

And so, "[a]t four thirty in the morning of April 12 a signal mortar sounded and a red ball ascended in a lazy curve to burst over the fort." "All day and into the rainy night the encircling batteries pounded at the fort"[24] and its Star-Spangled Banner. After a bombardment that lasted thirty-four hours, Fort Sumter surrendered.[25]

In the South, people cheered. But in the North—in the "Land of the Free and the Home of the Brave"—people rose in fury at the traitors who dared to fire upon the Star-Spangled Banner.[26]

Stephen Douglas raced to the White House. He pledged his support—and the support of all Democrats–to join with the Republicans to save the Union. Yet, at that very moment, Stephen Douglas was dying from cancer. To save the Union, he spent the last months of his life making speeches that rallied the North to fight for the Union that Abraham Lincoln and he both loved.[27]

No, Frederick Douglass didn't go to Haiti. Instead, he shouted, "God be praised!"[28]

Frederick Douglass did not rejoice because he liked war. Frederick Douglass rejoiced because he saw that war would bring liberty for his people.

Frederick Douglass rejoiced because he heard God's truth marching on. Frederick Douglass rejoiced because he understood that the Union could only be saved by granting liberty to those Americans who had come from Africa. Frederick Douglass rejoiced because he understood that Liberty *and* Union truly were one and inseparable, then and forever.

PART I: The Last, Best Hope of Humanity

ABRAHAM LINCOLN VERSUS GEORGE McCLELLAN

It took two years of bloody fighting before Abraham Lincoln realized that he could not save the Union without granting liberty to the slaves—that *Liberty and Union* truly were *one and inseparable, then and forever.*

During the first two years of the Civil War, the Union won hardly any battles—especially in the decisive battleground between the capital city of the Union (Washington) and the capital city of the Confederacy (Richmond).

In fact, these two cities were separated by less than a hundred miles. As Winston Churchill described it, "Thus the two capitols stood like queens at chess upon adjoining squares, and, sustained by their combinations of covering pieces, they endured four years of grim play within a single move of capture."[1]

For this reason, many of the famous Civil War battles were fought by Union armies advancing towards Richmond. The first such battle was Bull Run. When it occurred, each side had had only a few months to train its army. The battle began in an almost festive atmosphere—almost like a modern-day Super Bowl! Ladies and gentlemen rode out from Washington in carriages to see Union troops crush the rebels. Each side fully believed that it would whip the enemy in a glorious battle that would quickly decide the fate of the Union.

At first, the Union troops seemed to be winning. But Stonewall Jackson rallied his troops (he got his nickname by stopping the Union army in this battle "like a stone wall"). Then, fresh Confederate reinforcements arrived in the nick of time to turn near-defeat into victory. The "green" troops in the Union army became a panicked mob, fleeing back to Washington.[2]

With the benefit of hindsight, armchair quarterbacks have wondered why the Confederates didn't immediately march to Washington, occupy the Union capital, and win the war. Some of the answer is that the green *Confederate* troops were nearly as disorganized in their victory as the green Union troops were demoralized by their defeat.

Furthermore, Jefferson Davis, the President of the Confederacy, did not want to invade the North. He wanted to fight a defensive war,[3] emphasizing that the Confederacy only wanted to be left alone. He hoped that some combination of Yankee war weariness and European intervention to end the bloodshed would lead to the independence of the Confederacy. After all, George Washington used much the same strategy to win independence from the British Empire.

Meanwhile, to organize the defense of Washington and to train the Army of the Potomac that defended it, Lincoln chose General George B. McClellan. This short, well-dressed, incredibly talented man (the same characteristics that described Lincoln's old nemesis, Stephen Douglas) quickly showed the military flair of a new Napoleon.[4] At first, everyone sang his praises. Then doubts began to arise. McClellan kept training and planning instead of fighting. He was far better at making excuses than at making war.[5]

A frustrated Lincoln put it this way: "If by magic he could reinforce McClellan with 100,000 men today, he would be in an ecstasy over it, thank him for it, and tell him that he would go to Richmond tomorrow, but that when tomorrow came he would telegraph that he had certain information that the enemy had 400,000 men, and that he could not advance without reinforcements."[6]

The main problem seems to have been McClellan's personality. He was a brilliant staff officer. No one was better at training, fortifying, and planning. But he was not a man of action. He was a planner, not a doer.[7]

McClellan was also a Democrat. And in those days, when treason and rebellion were rampant, many Republicans suspected McClellan himself of treason. A fairer appraisal is that McClellan hoped, as did Democrats and many others across the North, that the Union could be saved without causing revolutionary upheavals such as the freeing of the slaves. The hope—as before Bull Run—was that one great victory in battle would end the rebellion. Then life could go on as it had before the rebels fired on Fort Sumter.

Such naive optimism and McClellan's excessive caution led to endless delays. Bull Run took place in July, 1861. But despite repeated urging by Lincoln (and by Congressional Republicans), McClellan did not launch an offensive during the rest of 1861. Then, McClellan went into winter quarters and frittered away the entire winter season.

Then, McClellan told Lincoln that he had a brilliant plan that was so secret that he shouldn't even tell the President—so, (amazingly) he didn't![8] It turned out that the secret plan was to load the Army of the Potomac onto boats and sail them to a spot about fifty miles from Richmond.[9]

Lincoln immediately voiced valid concerns, such as: this complicated maneuver would certainly lead to even more delays in fighting the enemy; Washington would be vulnerable to enemy attack; there would still be many miles between the army and Richmond, so what would be gained by shifting the battlefield at such expense and delay; and could the army be evacuated safely if it was defeated?[10]

McClellan had brilliant answers for each of Lincoln's fears, and so the enterprise went ahead. But Lincoln's instincts proved correct. Everything that he'd feared came true. By the time McClellan finished shipping the army south to the Peninsula, he wasn't able to start advancing towards Richmond until May third—about ten months after the last major battle at Bull Run.

The enemy knew all about McClellan's strategy well in advance, so Confederate troops were well dug-in. Nothing had been gained by sailing the Army down the coast. As Lincoln had predicted, the Union army faced the same well-fortified troops as if it had simply marched straight towards Richmond months earlier.

McClellan advanced cautiously towards Richmond, constantly making excuses for his tardiness. Meanwhile, Stonewall Jackson was busy in the Shenandoah Valley, out-marching and out-fighting the Union troops. In Washington, fears grew that Stonewall Jackson might be able to capture the Union capital. Troops were diverted from McClellan to defend Washington.[11]

Nevertheless, by the end of June, McClellan and his Army reached the outskirts of Richmond.[12] They were so close they could even hear Richmond's church bells ringing.[13]

McClellan sensed that victory was near. But then came one of those twists of fate that change history forever. In the fighting outside Richmond, the top Confederate general was seriously wounded. Jefferson Davis had to find a replacement. He turned to a general who hadn't performed very well in the early days of the war and so had been assigned to a "desk job" doing staff work.[14] The general's name was Robert E. Lee.

In a series of lightning-swift battles, Lee whipped McClellan. The Union army barely escaped destruction in this Battle of the Seven Days. When it was over, the Union Army huddled behind its powerful artillery at its base near the coast—cowed and demoralized.

The Union armies in the East were now divided between the forces with McClellan and the forces defending Washington. Lee struck north, hoping to win the South's independence by annihilating the Union armies defending Washington before McClellan could reinforce them.

Leaving a small screening force to contain the timid McClellan, Lee joined forces with the Confederate forces menacing Washington. In the Second Battle of Bull Run, Lee routed the Union army.[15]

In two months, Lee had driven the Yankees from the gates of Richmond to the gates of Washington. No wonder the South worshipped Lee as their greatest hero!

In contrast, the North was distraught. Daniel Webster's worst nightmare was coming true. As far back as 1830, this matchless orator of the North had feared:

"When my eyes shall be turned to behold for the last time the sun in heaven, may I not see him shining on the broken and dishonored fragments of a once-glorious Union; on States dissevered, discordant, belligerent; on a land rent with civil feuds, or drenched, it may be, in fraternal blood."[16]

But now, "[t]he state of the Union . . . was critical in the extreme." The "demoralized and badly whipped" Union troops were "retiring toward Washington in disorder, with thousands of stragglers clogging the roads." No one was in control.

"Fearing that Lee would descend upon the capital, Lincoln . . . felt little confidence that [he] could save the distracted city."[17] In this crisis, there was only one man to whom Lincoln could turn—McClellan. No one else had the skill to meet the need. No one else could inspire the Army of the Potomac except this man whom they adored—McClellan.

And so came another one of those twists of fate that change history forever. The matchless prose of the Civil War historian, Bruce Catton, best captures the drama of that historic moment:

> It became a legend . . . how McClellan this one time rose to a great challenge and met it fully. He was a small man, and he missed many chances . . . ; but for one evening of his life he was great . . . McClellan rode out from Alexandria on his great black war horse, a jaunty little man with a yellow sash around his waist, every pose and gesture perfect. He cantered down the dusty roads and he met the heads of the retreating columns, and he cried words of encouragement and swung his little cap, and he gave the beaten men what no other man alive could have given them—enthusiasm, hope, confidence, an exultant and unreasoning feeling that the time of troubles was over and that everything would be all right now. And it went into the legend—truthfully, for many men have testified to it—that down mile after mile of Virginia roads the stumbling columns came alive, and threw caps and knapsacks into the air, and yelled until they could yell no more, and went on doing it until the sun went down; and after dark, exhausted men who lay in the dust sprang to their feet and cried aloud because they saw this dapper little rider outlined against the purple starlight.[18]

Within a few days, McClellan beat Robert E. Lee at the Battle of Antietam—the most brutal slugfest of the entire war. About 20,000 men were killed or wounded in a single day.[19]

McClellan saved the Union. But he did not save himself from being fired a few months later.

What happened? McClellan was fired because he wasted this golden opportunity to win the Civil War. On the day of battle, McClellan did not commit his last reserves to the fray—he held back fresh troops who would surely have overwhelmed the out-gunned and exhausted Confederate troops. Instead, McClellan gave Lee the chance he needed to pull his battered army together.

The next day, McClellan failed to attack Lee's badly mauled army as it lay prostrate before him with its back to Antietam Creek, giving Lee the chance he needed to retreat south that night.

Then, McClellan failed to pursue Lee south, dogging his every step . . . the way that Ulysses S. Grant would relentlessly pursue Lee two years later . . . until Lee surrendered. Instead, true to McClellan's cautious, procrastinating nature, he rested, and trained his army.[20]

Lincoln could not believe it!

By late October (more than a month after the battle of Antietam on September 17), McClellan was claiming that his horses were "absolutely broken down from fatigue and want of flesh." Lincoln was so exasperated with this latest excuse for inaction that he replied: "Will you pardon me for asking what the horses of your army have done since the Battle of Antietam that fatigue anything?"[21]

Lincoln could not endure it. And Lincoln did not tolerate it. After waiting in vain until after the elections in November for McClellan to attack Lee, Lincoln fired him.[22] McClellan never commanded an army again. The cautious general had saved the Union. But it would never be the same Union.

Because—unlike McClellan, but *like* George Washington when he crossed the Delaware—Abraham Lincoln made bold moves to win wars. Therefore, after the emotional lift from the Union victory at Antietam, Lincoln announced his decision to free the slaves.

Because—unlike McClellan, but *like* Christopher Columbus—Abraham Lincoln took great risks to win great gains. Lincoln took the risk that the support of bold visionaries (such as Harriett Beecher Stowe and Frederick Douglass) would outweigh the complaining of cautious fence-sitters (such as McClellan). He also gambled that freeing the slaves would keep Britain from intervening in the war.

Although British intervention to obtain a "truce" might appear to be even-handed, such intervention would actually have ensured that the Confederacy became independent. By 1862, the only way to restore the South to the Union was to conquer the South by continuing the war. Emotions ran high, and already, enough Southern blood had been shed that there was no way that the South would voluntarily return to the Union.

Indeed, there were several reasons why Britain would benefit by intervening to end the war. A noble motive would be to end bloodshed. A purely economic motive would be to restore the flow of cotton that British textile mills needed. A Machiavellian motive would be to weaken America by dividing it into two countries.

Furthermore, before the Union victory at Antietam, it was beginning to appear as if a Confederate victory in the war was inevitable. Not only had Lee whipped the Union Army on the East Coast, but another Confederate Army had driven the Yankees out of Tennessee, and was advancing into Kentucky.[23]

Indeed, the British Prime Minister tentatively decided to mediate the conflict. In a speech by a leading member of the British government, the rationale for such intervention was explained, enraging the North with a prediction that the North would lose the war and that the South had already succeeded in establishing a new nation:

> We know quite well that the people of the Northern states have not yet drunk of the cup—they are still trying to hold it from their lips—which all the world sees they nevertheless must drink of. We may have our own opinions about slavery, we may be for or against the South, but there is no doubt that Jefferson Davis and other leaders of the South have made an Army; they are making, it appears, a Navy; and they have made what is more than either; they have made a Nation.[24]

Despite such rhetoric, the reality was that once the American Civil War became a war to free the slaves, no British government could intervene to help the slaveholders of the South. Under Queen Victoria, Christian England couldn't bear such a blight on its conscience.

Therefore, Lincoln decided by July of 1862 that he must free the slaves. He even drafted an Emancipation Proclamation. But he knew that he could not take this bold step when the Union armies were in disarray and the Confederates were triumphant. It would look too much like an act of desperation. So, until the Union could win a battle, Lincoln put away the piece of paper that would free the slaves.[25]

At this darkest moment of supreme crisis, McClellan won the battle of Antietam. Lincoln was now able to free the slaves and save the Union. But the Union that was saved by Abraham Lincoln would never be the same as the Union that existed before the Civil War—that hypocritical Union that achieved unity by compromising liberty—by refusing to see, hear, and understand the evils of human slavery.

The Union that was saved by the bloodshed of the Civil War became a Union whose purpose was to guarantee liberty for *all* people–even for the long-enslaved descendants of Africans. Thanks, ironically, to George McClellan, the Union that was saved by Abraham Lincoln became inseparable from winning liberty for all people–liberty for all Humanity—both then and forevermore.

ABRAHAM LINCOLN VERSUS ROBERT E. LEE

It took two more years of bloody fighting before Robert E. Lee realized that liberty and union truly were one and inseparable, then and forevermore. This officer and gentleman embodied all that was best about the Old South. Robert E. Lee deplored slavery. He loved the Union. But Robert E. Lee loved his homeland, Virginia, even more. So he came to Virginia's defense when duty called.[1]

Virginia shared the conviction of the South that it had the same right to leave the Union as the original colonies had had to leave the British Empire. Indeed, the South felt that the best, the ultimate, safeguard of liberty was the right of a state to leave the Union if tyranny by the federal government threatened the unalienable rights of people to life, liberty, and the pursuit of happiness.

This belief was plausible, but misguided. As James Madison explained in *The Federalist, No. X* in 1787 (during the debate whether to ratify the United States Constitution) people's rights and liberties are far more secure in a large republic than in a small republic. This brilliant insight of political science rested on Madison's realization that it is far easier to establish a tyranny by a majority if only a small, homogeneous group needs to act in unison. As Madison explained:

> The smaller the society, the fewer probably will be the distinct parties and interests composing it; . . . and the smaller the compass within which they are placed, the more easily will they concert and execute their plans of oppression. Extend the sphere, and . . . you make it less probable that a majority of the whole will have a common motive to invade the rights of other citizens [or be able] to act in unison with each other.

One example of Madison's insight was the establishment of freedom of religion in the United States. In colonial times, individual colonies had different "established religions." For example, Congregationalists were strong in Massachusetts and Episcopalians were strong in Virginia. When these diverse states joined the same Union, it was impossible to establish a single religion for the entire United States.

Another example of Madison's insight was the ending of legalized segregation in the South during the 1950s and 1960s. Because African-Americans could appeal to the consciences of whites outside of the South, they were able to overcome the localized tyranny of whites within the South.

A vestige of this wisdom of that great Virginian, James Madison, remained in the Virginia of 1861. Therefore, unlike South Carolina and the other states in the Deep South, Virginia and the other states in the Upper South did not leave the Union merely because Abraham Lincoln was elected President.

Instead, Virginia and these other Southern states waited to see if Lincoln would actually resort to tyranny against the South. When Lincoln tried to coerce the Confederate States back into the Union after Fort Sumter fell, these Southern states decided that they must fight to preserve this fundamental safeguard of their Liberties—the right to leave the Union in order to thwart tyranny.

Robert E. Lee gave his first loyalty to his home state, Virginia, instead of to the Union—much as people today give their first loyalty to the United States of America instead of to the United Nations. Therefore, when Virginia decided to leave the Union, Robert E. Lee resigned his commission in the United States Army and volunteered to defend his homeland, Virginia, by becoming a general in the Confederate Army.

We have already seen how brilliantly Robert E. Lee drove the "Yankees" from the gates of Richmond. But he was admired for far more than his military skills. In his wisdom, in his integrity, and in his determination to defend the liberties of his homeland, Robert E. Lee was the equal of George Washington himself.[2]

Robert E. Lee's failure to become the father of a new nation is primarily due to the fact that instead of fighting the foolish, corrupt and tyrannical King George III, Lee fought someone whose wisdom, integrity, and determination to defend the liberties of his homeland were unsurpassed by Lee or Washington: Abraham Lincoln.

With Lincoln's Emancipation Proclamation, the best hope of Confederate independence—intervention from Britain—was lost. Now, all depended on Lee winning independence on the field of battle—either by annihilating the Union Army that was defending Washington or by holding out until war weariness in the North made them quit.

Lincoln looked for a general to beat Lee. In General Burnside, he hoped he'd found the answer, but he was mistaken. Like a loyal dog, Burnside followed Lincoln's order to attack Lee too narrow-mindedly. He marched straight toward Richmond and ran into a buzz saw at Fredericksburg. Even though the Confederates were fortified on high ground, Burnside foolishly sent his army charging uphill. The well-entrenched Confederates slaughtered the brave Union troops. After this bloody defeat, Burnside sent his army back to their barracks until spring.[3]

The situation was so bad that some people feared—and other people hoped—that Lincoln would change his mind about freeing the slaves. This possibility existed because the Emancipation Proclamation that Lincoln issued on September 22, 1862, was merely a *preliminary* Emancipation Proclamation. It took the form of a warning to the rebels that, unless they surrendered by January 1, 1863, Lincoln would free their slaves on that date.

This two-step approach made sense considering the legal basis on which Lincoln relied to free the slaves. Normally, the President would not have the power to take away property from a United States citizen–not even a toothpick–without fair compensation after due process as guaranteed by the Fifth Amendment to the Constitution. But during a war, the President has the power, as commander in chief of the military, to do many things that he could not do in peacetime in order to win the war.

One special wartime authority afforded to the President is the power to take property away from the enemy so that the enemy's war effort is weakened. Usually, this might mean confiscating their horses so that their cavalry would have no horses. But this time, the President said that he would take away their slaves, arguing that he had the power to take this immense step as one of his war powers as commander in chief.

To show that he was taking this extraordinary step solely as a wartime measure, Lincoln gave the South a few months to make peace before his proclamation took effect. Then, according to the preliminary Emancipation Proclamation, Lincoln would issue a final Emancipation Proclamation on January 1, 1863, freeing the slaves of anyone who remained in rebellion on that date.[4]

The South did not make peace. Instead, the Republicans suffered major losses in that fall's elections, due in part to people's anger that Lincoln was converting "a war to save the Union" into "a war to free the slaves."

Staunch abolitionists were also disillusioned with Lincoln. They complained that Lincoln was only going to free the slaves in areas where his action would not take effect because Confederate forces remained in control. (Lincoln could not, or at least *did not,* use his special wartime powers to free slaves in states that had remained loyal to the Union, such as Kentucky and Maryland, or in areas of the South such as New Orleans where Union troops were in control.)

Indeed, during the period between issuing the preliminary Emancipation Proclamation and making it final, "Lincoln's leadership was more seriously threatened than at any other time, and it was not clear that his administration could survive the repeated crises that it faced."[5]

How did Lincoln find the strength and courage to go on? His vision of America strengthened him. And his faith in America encouraged him. In his annual message to Congress on December 1, 1862, Lincoln wrote: "In times like the present, men should utter nothing for which they would not willingly be responsible through time and eternity." Lincoln knew that "[t]he dogmas of the quiet past are inadequate to the stormy present." Although "[t]he occasion is piled high with difficulty, . . . we must rise with the occasion." "[W]e must think anew and act anew."

Lincoln exhorted: "Fellow citizens, we cannot escape history . . . The fiery trial through which we pass will light us down in honor or dishonor to the last generation."

Lincoln prophesied: "in giving freedom to the slave, we assure freedom to the free–honorable alike in what we give and what we preserve." Lincoln warned: "We shall nobly save or meanly lose the last, best hope of earth."

But so long as Robert E. Lee fought on so gallantly, the last, best hope of earth—the last, best hope of Humanity—was in danger of being snuffed out forever. Indeed, merely two weeks after these inspirational words from Lincoln came the depressing news of the bloody, bungled defeat at Fredericksburg—further weakening the President's supporters and strengthening his detractors.

Small wonder that African-Americans feared Lincoln would not carry through on his promise to free the slaves. "To most liberals and militant black leaders, the president was something of an enigma; a good man, to be sure, honest, decent, and kind, but slow, timid, vacillating even, in his approach to the supreme moral issue of the age. As the moment of truth approached, many people said Lincoln would never go through with it."[6]

Therefore, Frederick Douglass and other friends of liberty waited nervously at a gathering in Boston on New Year's Day, longing for the good news from Washington that Lincoln had freed the slaves.

Hours dragged by. Still no telegram arrived.

Unbeknownst to the fretting crowd in Boston, the signing ceremony for the Emancipation Proclamation had been delayed because Lincoln was tied up at a New Year's Ball. But at last, at 10 p.m., the crowd in Boston learned that a telegram had come from Washington. It was finished!!! The slaves were free!!!

Suddenly everyone standing with Frederick Douglass was "shouting, laughing, weeping."[7] And far away, on islands off South Carolina that Union troops were occupying, blacks and whites celebrated in a grove of giant oaks. When the Union commander unfolded a new flag, "an old dry voice came from the audience. The old man carried it by himself for a little while. Then two women joined in and another man and another until the words swelled out:

> My country, 'tis of thee,
> Sweet land of liberty,
> Of thee I sing.

The Union commander said later: "I never saw anything so electric; it made all other words cheap. It seemed the choked voice of a race at last unloosed."[8]

To make this promise of liberty come true, however, Lincoln must still defeat Robert E. Lee—a formidable task that was bungled once again in the spring of 1863. This time the bungler was General Joe Hooker, nicknamed "Fightin' Joe." Cocky and bold, he boasted that he led the finest army on the planet. This boast may even have been true. The army that he led was twice the size of Robert E. Lee's army.

Nevertheless, Lee quickly outflanked Hooker's army at the Battle of Chancellorsville. The Yankees fled north, happy that they hadn't been annihilated.

Then Lee made his boldest gamble of the war. He knew that the South was weakening beneath the hammer blows of the larger, economically stronger Union. He must win *now*, or watch the slow collapse of the South beneath the awesome resources of the Union. And so, Lee marched north, seeking to win an overwhelming victory in a battle on Northern soil that he hoped would force the North to give up.[9]

Lee's advancing army collided with the Union army at Gettysburg. For three desperate days, the future of America hung in the balance as Lee tried to overcome the immense odds against him.

On the eve of battle, Lincoln replaced Hooker with General Meade who, in this crisis, "led" essentially by chairing a committee of the army's generals. They did nothing—except order their troops to hold on, but at least they did no harm—a far better result than the constant blundering of McClellan, Burnside, and Hooker.

This time it was Robert E. Lee who blundered. As Winston Churchill later wrote, "Lee believed that his own army was invincible, and . . . he had begun to regard the [Union Army] almost with contempt. He failed to distinguish between bad troops and good troops badly led."[10] Deceived by his pride in his army and in himself, Lee marched to defeat at Gettysburg.

After two days of bloody fighting, Lee had not overcome the Union Army. He should have retreated. But like a quarterback who makes a desperate pass late in a key game and gets intercepted, Lee made a last, desperate attack to try to win the battle—and the war. We remember this last, desperate bid for victory as Pickett's Charge.

Pickett's Charge is synonymous with bravery—and *futility*. Fifteen thousand of Robert E. Lee's best troops waved their flags, yelled their defiance, and marched gallantly into a blizzard of metal spewing forth from rows of Yankee cannons defending the high ground at Cemetery Ridge. As Churchill described it: "In splendid array, all their battle flags flying, the forlorn assault marched on. But . . . they faced odds and metal beyond the virtue of mortals. . . . Less than a third came back."[11]

But the greatest Union victory at Gettysburg was not won with guns. The greatest Union victory at Gettysburg was won with words—the immortal words of Abraham Lincoln in "The Gettysburg Address."

Four months after the battle, Lincoln spoke at Gettysburg during a ceremony held to dedicate a cemetery to the slain soldiers. Lincoln wasn't the main speaker. Nevertheless, he spoke words that have captured the imagination of Americans and Humanity ever since.

Lincoln reminded people that America was "a new nation, conceived in liberty, and dedicated to the proposition that all men are created equal." He honored those who "gave their lives that that nation might live." He called on the living to be "dedicated to the great task remaining before us."

What was this great task? To give America "under God, . . . a new birth of freedom" so that "government of the people, by the people, for the people, shall not perish from the earth."

Against such a vision of America, not even the skill of Robert E. Lee could prevail. Especially not against the skill and determination of General Ulysses S. Grant.

At virtually the same moment that the South lost the battle of Gettysburg, General Grant completed the conquest of the Mississippi River by capturing the city of Vicksburg, Mississippi. Later in 1863, Grant smashed the Confederate Army in Tennessee, driving the Confederates back to Georgia.

Lincoln now put Grant in charge of all of the Union armies. By the spring of 1864, the Union at last had a general worthy of the brave men he led.

Grant outnumbered Lee by two-to-one. Therefore, even though Grant could never overcome Lee's genius in battle, he gradually ground Lee and the South into the dust. Grant's soulmate in this war of attrition was General Sherman, who advanced relentlessly toward Atlanta.

The South's last hope was that Lincoln might not be re-elected in the Presidential election scheduled for the fall of 1864.

The Democrats dusted off General McClellan to run against his old nemesis, Abraham Lincoln. There was little doubt that if the Democrats and McClellan won the election, they would make peace with the South, establishing the Confederacy as an independent nation.

At one point in 1864, it looked as if Lincoln would indeed lose the election. The North was appalled at the human sacrifice of Grant's constant battles against Lee. The most horrible blood-letting came at the battle of Cold Harbor, where 7,000 Union troops died in about an hour making a fruitless, misguided attempt to charge well-entrenched Confederates.

Despite this bungled battle that was reminiscent of Burnside's foolish assault at Fredericksburg, Grant fought on. By August, he had pinned Lee into trenches south of Richmond. Meanwhile, Sherman was held up besieging Atlanta. To a war-weary North that was sickened by the endless slaughter, it appeared that the South could never be beaten.[12]

But then, in early September, came the break that Lincoln needed. Sherman captured Atlanta. It was now clear to everyone that the South could not survive much longer. The North rallied behind Lincoln and he won the election by a large margin.[13]

That winter, Sherman made his infamous "March To The Sea,"—the campaign that is immortalized in Gone With The Wind. To break the backbone of the South and to cripple its ability to continue the war, Sherman spread destruction from Atlanta to Savannah, destroying buildings, animals, homes, and crops.

When Lincoln gave his Second Inaugural Address, the victory of the Union was expected within a few months. Thus he said, "Fondly do we hope, fervently do we pray, that this mighty scourge of war may speedily pass away."

Lincoln struggled to find a rationale for the horrible plague of bloodshed that had struck America during four years of "brother fighting brother." He blamed both the North *and* the South for the debacle. Because slavery was "somehow, the cause of the war" and *both* the North and the South had tolerated slavery and benefitted from it for many years—in fact, nearly 250 years. Therefore, God, Who is just, gave "to both North and South, this terrible war, as the woe due to those" who had enslaved others.

As terrible as God's judgment had been thus far, who could know whether even more horrors might lie ahead? Because, said Lincoln, "if God wills that [this mighty scourge of war] continue until all the wealth piled by the bondsman's two hundred and fifty years of unrequited toil shall be sunk, and until every drop of blood drawn with the lash shall be paid by another drawn with the sword, as was said three thousand years ago, so still it must be said, 'The judgments of the Lord are true and righteous altogether.'"

After this horrifying confession of America's sin and guilt, Lincoln ended on a more hopeful note. His gaze shifted from God punishing America for its sins toward God blessing America in the future. Abraham Lincoln gave us a vision of America that could bring peace between North and South, and peace for all Humanity.

His vision of peace did not rely on revenge and retribution. Instead, he urged Americans to achieve a just and lasting peace "[w]ith malice toward none, with charity for all, [and] with firmness in the right as God gives us to see the right."

In this spirit of forgiveness, love, and righteousness, said Lincoln, America should "strive on to finish the work we are in, to bind up the nation's wounds, to care for him who shall have borne the battle and for his widow and his orphan, to do all which may achieve and cherish a just and lasting peace among ourselves and with all nations."

When we hear such wisdom, we know that Mrs. Lincoln was right when she said that her husband's heart was as large as his arms were long.[14] Because to confess sins, to forgive others, and to work towards a glorious future of peace for all Humanity, you must have the heart of Jesus Christ—the largest heart of all.

Tragically, Abraham Lincoln did not live long enough to "achieve and cherish a just and lasting peace among ourselves and with all nations." He lived long enough to see Robert E. Lee surrender on Palm Sunday.[15] But, like Jesus Christ, Abraham Lincoln was killed a few days later, on Good Friday, at the hands of scheming evildoers.[16]

Also like Jesus Christ, Lincoln achieved by his death what he could not have achieved any other way. As a martyr for America, Lincoln's words and wisdom achieved a sanctity that has guided America ever since.

Lincoln had the wisdom to see America's sins, to hear America's sins, and to understand America's sins. Lincoln had the wisdom to know that, as the prophet Isaiah had explained 2,500 years earlier, if we see our sins, hear our sins, and understand our sins, God will enable us to turn from our sins and God will heal our land (Isaiah 6:9–10). Furthermore, Lincoln had the wisdom to perceive that, after we confess our sins, God enables us to see and to do what is right (1 John 1:5–9).

We can see that Harriett Beecher Stowe was right when she warned, in *Uncle Tom's Cabin*, that "[b]oth North and South have been guilty before God" and that the Union could not be saved "by combining together, to protect injustice and cruelty."

We can see that Harriett Beecher Stowe was right when she prophesied that the Union could only be saved "by repentance, justice, and mercy." These were the key themes of Lincoln's Second Inaugural Address, urging Americans to repent of the sin of slavery, to be just to the freed slaves, and to be merciful to their enemies.

Furthermore, as Lincoln well understood, to atone for America's sins, she must "achieve a just and lasting peace among ourselves and with all nations."

America must come in peace for all Humanity.

And the only way to come in peace for all Humanity is "[w]ith malice toward none, with charity for all, [and] with firmness in the right as God gives us to see the right."

CHAPTER 4

Peace for All Humanity

Susan B. Anthony

ONE OF FREDERICK DOUGLASS'S FRIENDS, when he lived in Rochester, New York, was Susan B. Anthony. Her name stands as tall in the annals of freedom for women as *his* name stands tall in the annals of freedom for African-Americans.

Susan B. Anthony's most memorable blow for women's rights was struck in the presidential election of 1872. These years immediately after the Civil War were full of both turmoil and possibility. The former slaves were now voting in the South—electing African-Americans to Congress and to governor's mansions.

Susan B. Anthony wondered, "If former slaves can vote, why can't women vote?" To dramatize her point, she registered to vote for President in 1872. Former General Ulysses S. Grant was running for a second term.

Grant had never fought an enemy as powerful as men's prejudice against women. For daring to vote, Susan B. Anthony was arrested, convicted, and fined $100.

Fortunately, Susan B. Anthony was as persistent fighting prejudice as General Grant had been persistent fighting Robert E. Lee. She never gave in as she fought prejudice to prove that God created all *people* equal, not just all *men* equal. She never gave in as she fought prejudice so that women could enjoy life, liberty, and the pursuit of happiness.

CUSTER'S LAST STAND

In his Second Inaugural Address, Lincoln envisioned an America that achieved and cherished "a just and lasting peace . . . with all nations." Unfortunately, this vision of America was as far from being fulfilled as Susan B. Anthony's vision of women having the same rights as men.

Nowhere was the gap between America's rhetoric of making peace and its reality of making war greater than in the destruction of Native Americans after the Civil War. In fact, the restored Union used the same methods to crush the Native Americans as the Union had used to crush the Confederacy. The immense resources of the Union were applied relentlessly until the new "enemy's" army was destroyed and his ancient way of life was "gone with the wind."

Ironically, one of the few victories of Native Americans in their desperate struggle for freedom was against a flamboyant, popular Civil War general, George Armstrong Custer. In June of 1876, Custer was leading a regiment of cavalry out West in a war against the Sioux. Arrogantly, he miscalculated the size and cleverness of his enemy. Finally, the Sioux surrounded and killed Custer and 264 of his men.

The United States responded to news of the disaster the same way that the United States always responds to news of a defeat—be it the loss of the Alamo, the loss of Fort Sumter, or the destruction of its fleet at Pearl Harbor. The war is pursued with even greater resources and resolve until total victory is secured.

And so it was against the defenseless Native Americans. Despite adroit "guerilla warfare" strategies and impassioned war cries, the bow and arrow had little power against rifle and cannon fire.

Within a few years, the buffalo herds that the tribes depended upon for their survival were gone—slaughtered to deprive the

Native Americans of this key resource. By 1890, buffalo were almost an extinct species.

Military resistance was futile. The United States sent larger armies so that a debacle such as Custer's Last Stand would never happen again.

Within a few years, the once-mighty, freedom-loving tribes of the Great Plains were penned into Indian Reservations, where their humiliated and despised people fell into depression and despair.

THE ELECTION OF 1876

1876 marked the 100th anniversary of the Declaration of Independence. Ironically, 1876 not only marked the hopelessness of Native Americans after their fleeting victory at Custer's Last Stand—1876 also marked a disastrous setback for African-Americans in their struggle for equal rights to life, liberty, and the pursuit of happiness.

During the first decade after the Civil War, the Federal Government and the Union Army ran the political machine in the South. Compared to the end of most civil wars, the South was treated gently. Not even the South's leading general, Robert E. Lee, nor the Confederacy's President, Jefferson Davis, were executed. Lincoln's vision of reconciliation based on malice toward none and charity for all was largely carried out.

Nevertheless, the South groaned beneath the agony of economic collapse and political castration. Most white Southerners lost the right to vote because they had rebelled against the United States. But former slaves could vote. Therefore, "the last became first and the first became last." For over a decade, the South's traditional aristocracy lost power to its former slaves.

This reversal of roles could only continue as long as the North was willing to spend huge sums of money to help the former slaves and was willing to risk another civil war by deploying the Union Army in the South. The Presidential Election of 1876 marked the end of such intervention by the North in the Southern states.

Although the Election of 1876 was amazingly close, any fair count of the votes would have elected the Democratic candidate for President, Samuel J. Tilden.[1] However, the Republican Party still controlled several key Southern states. Through corrupt practices, the Republicans tampered with the vote count to elect their candidate, Rutherford B. Hayes.

The nation deadlocked, unable to decide which man was truly the next President of the United States. There was even some chance that a *new* civil war could break out. However, the bloodletting of the Civil War was so fresh in people's minds that the Republicans and Democrats found a way of compromising instead of fighting.

We have seen that, prior to the Civil War, whites had compromised several times to preserve the Union at the expense of black people who were left to suffer in slavery. The Missouri Compromise and the Compromise of 1850 were the most famous of these compromises.

The essence of the compromise after the Election of 1876 was that, in exchange for the Republican candidate becoming the next President, the Union Army would be withdrawn from all Southern states and the North would stop interfering with the "internal affairs" of the South.

Once again, the big losers in the Compromise were African-Americans, who were essentially re-enslaved. Economically, they were tied to their former masters by debts and customs. Segregation of the races was enforced by the terror of the Ku Klux Klan and the power of new "Jim Crow" laws.

How could this happen? Why did the North turn its back on African-Americans?

The North's abandonment and betrayal of the freed slaves is much easier to understand if you remember that the North did not begin the Civil War in order to free the slaves. The North began the Civil War in order to save the Union after the rebels dared to fire upon the Star-Spangled Banner at Fort Sumter. It was only as a last resort to help win the resulting civil war that Lincoln mustered the personal courage and the political strength to free the South's slaves.

Furthermore, virtually no whites believed in racial equality. Although many northern whites thought that slavery was wrong, this did not change their ingrained racist certainty that whites were superior to blacks.

Writing in 1855, Frederick Douglass noted the "American prejudice against color" and described how he "found this prejudice very strong and very annoying" when he traveled in New England. Indeed, Douglass found that "[t]he abolitionists themselves were not entirely free from [such racial prejudice, although he] could see that they were nobly struggling against it." When they were children, they "had all been educated to believe that if they were bad, the old *black* man—not the old *devil*—would get them . . ." Thus, even the noblest abolitionists found it hard "to get the better of their fears." For example, they betrayed their ingrained racial fears when they would say to him, "Mr. Douglass, I will walk to meeting with you; I am not afraid of a black man."[2]

Abraham Lincoln was not an abolitionist and he shared the racist preconceptions of his age about blacks being inferior to whites. When pressed for a solution about what to do about freed slaves, he deluded himself with fantastic schemes about sending the blacks back to Africa.[3]

White fantasies about sending the blacks back to Africa betrayed the same old white habit of not seeing the problems of racism, not hearing the problems of racism, and not understanding the problems of racism.

Truthfully, the pattern was set by the way men treated women. Although men wanted women in their beds and in their kitchens, they didn't want them in the workplace or in the voting booth. Therefore, women were forced to slave away at home so that men wouldn't have to see, hear, or endeavor to understand them any place else.

Native Americans were forced onto reservations so that whites wouldn't have to see, hear, or endeavor to understand them. So if blacks wouldn't go away, why not segregate them, using Jim Crow laws in the South and using social pressure in the North? That way whites wouldn't have to see blacks, hear blacks, or understand blacks.

In retrospect, it seems amazing that more blacks didn't welcome the chance to leave a land that had treated them so terribly. An African-American historian gives us insight into why African-Americans love America so much that they stay in and serve America so faithfully:

> Why didn't they give up the struggle and go elsewhere? The answer is stunning in its simplicity: they believed in the *real* America, the one that was dreamed and betrayed. Their forefathers, they said, had settled the land and "manured it" with blood. The land was theirs, the country was theirs—they were willing to fight for it.[4]

Their vision of America gave them the courage and the determination to remain Americans no matter what the cost. Why should this surprise us?

It doesn't surprise us that descendants of those who arrived in the Mayflower want to stay in America because it is their home. So why should we be surprised that descendants of those who began arriving *before* the Mayflower want to stay in America because it is their home?

It doesn't surprise us that descendants of those who lived in America when the Declaration of Independence and the Constitution were written want to serve America because they are proud of their homeland. Almost every African-American is descended from such people because the slave trade ended in the early 1800s. So why should we be surprised that African-Americans want to serve America because they are proud of their homeland?

In fact, it is *not* surprising—it is *inspiring*—that African-Americans are patriotic, flag-waving Americans who still sing proudly the song that they sang in celebration on the day that Abraham Lincoln freed the slaves:

My country, 'tis of thee,
    Sweet land of liberty,
Of thee I sing.[5]

THE STATUE OF LIBERTY

In 1876, the people of France wanted to do something to show their friendship for America and to honor the 100th birthday of the Declaration of Independence. They remembered that great Frenchmen such as Lafayette had fought by the side of George Washington.

Moreover, the people of France were proud that their help—especially the presence of their army and fleet at Yorktown—was indispensable to America's victory in its war for independence.

And the people of France were grateful for the inspiration that the successful American Revolution had given to their own struggle for "Liberty, Equality, and Fraternity."

Therefore, the people of France donated money for a gift to America. And the artistic genius of France inspired the French sculptor Frederic Bartholdi to design a statue that was originally called "Liberty Enlightening the World."

In this vision of America, "Liberty" is a beautiful woman, lifting the Torch of Liberty towards the heavens. But Rome wasn't built in a day. Nor was the Statue of Liberty. It took until 1886 to erect the massive statue on a small island in the harbor of New York City.

As the years passed, the Statue of Liberty greeted millions of immigrants when they reached America's "golden shores." Her shining Torch of Liberty gave them hope for the Future as they beheld the coastline of America for the first time. In 1903, American poet Emma Lazarus engraved her vision of America on the Statue of Liberty:

Give me your tired, your poor,
Your huddled masses yearning to breathe free,
The wretched refuse of your teeming shore.

Send these, the homeless, tempest-tost to me,
I lift my lamp beside the golden door.

Lazarus' vision of America was the same vision that existed in the hearts of those who first discovered America—those who had first seen America with their hearts: Abraham, Moses, and Jesus. Abraham saw America when he left behind his homeland to seek a land where all people would be blessed.

Moses saw America when he told Pharaoh to let his people go free. Jesus saw America when he told us to be good neighbors—Good Samaritans who bind the wounds of those in need even though we have been taught to hate them because of their race, their nation, or their religion.

And *we* see America every time that we see the Torch of Liberty shining in the hearts of people everywhere.

"LAFAYETTE, WE ARE HERE"

In 1917, the people of America wanted to do something to show their friendship for France.

The people of America remembered that great Frenchmen such as Lafayette had fought by the side of George Washington. They were grateful that French help—especially the presence of their army and fleet at Yorktown—was indispensable to America's victory in its war for independence.

And the people of America were proud that the successful American Revolution had inspired the French in their own struggle for "Liberty, Equality, and Fraternity."

Therefore, the people of America gave the lives of their children to keep France free.

By 1917, France had been fighting desperately for three years against German invaders. Hundreds of miles of trenches crisscrossed the French countryside, demarcating the front line of the Great War.

By 1917, the French Army was bled white by three years of fruitless, senseless bloodshed. Some units were mutinous. They could no longer be depended upon to defend themselves, much less to attack the Germans and drive them from France.

By 1917, France's great ally, Russia, was wracked by revolution, crippling its war effort and ultimately leading to the rise of Communism, peace between Germany and Russia, and massive German attacks on France beginning in the Spring of 1918.

France's other great ally, Britain, fought valiantly on. But even the strength of her mighty, worldwide empire was ebbing. German submarines threatened to strangle the ship-borne commerce on which Britain's life depended.

In this desperate hour, America at last joined the Allies: Britain and France.

For three years, America had done her best to stay out of the butchery of the Great War. Indeed, President Woodrow Wilson won re-election in 1916 using the slogan: "He kept us out of war."[1]

America's traditional refusal to be drawn into Europe's wars stemmed from George Washington himself. In his Farewell Address, Washington warned against entangling alliances. He counseled that America should concentrate on *building* her strength through peace instead of *wasting* her strength on war.

Furthermore, America had strong ties to Germany. Millions of Americans, including my own father's ancestors, came from Germany. And a German, Baron von Steuben, had played a key role in training the American army during the Revolutionary War.

By contrast, Britain had been the traditional enemy of the United States throughout most of its existence. The Revolutionary War was fought against the British. In the War of 1812, the British burned the new capital at Washington, D.C., including the White House! During the Civil War, Britain had nearly intervened on the side of the *Confederacy* to weaken America forever.

Winston Churchill recalled that, as a young soldier in 1895, he had half-expected to fight the United States in a war over the boundary line between Venezuela and British Guiana.[2]

However, British propaganda was far more skillful than German propaganda. And the Germans foolishly gave the British plenty of ways to make Germany look like a barbaric aggressor.

For example, Kaiser Wilhelm and his Prussians alienated America early in the war with their invasion of neutral Belgium. Such a flagrant treaty violation marked Germany as an aggressor who would stop at nothing to conquer other nations, even those neutral countries, such as Belgium and the United States, which longed to remain at peace.

The burning and sacking of the medieval city Louvain, with its incomparable, irreplaceable library,[3] strengthened the view that modern Germans were no better than the German barbarians who destroyed the Roman Empire. Recalling Western Europe's ancient terror of barbarian invasions from the east, the Germans were called "the Huns."[4]

German submarines sank ships such as the Lusitania, causing the loss of innocent lives and undermining freedom of the seas.

Germany's clumsy efforts to entice Mexico to fight against America by promising that Mexico would recover lands lost in its war with the United States in the 1840s became known, enraging the United States and fanning fears of Germany. As the war progressed, America became more and more tied economically to the Allies. A blockade prevented commerce with Germany, but business boomed with the Allies. How would the Allies repay their loans if they lost the war?

At last, safely re-elected as President because he kept America *out* of war, Woodrow Wilson felt free to bring America *into* the war, and he quickly did so. The final straws were a renewal of attacks by German submarines against American ships and news of Germany's efforts to encourage Mexico to fight against the United States.

American idealism proclaimed that America was fighting to make the world safe for democracy. (At that moment, this goal was especially inspiring because the Russians had just established a democratic government—the one that the Communists soon overthrew.)

America would fight this one last "war to end all wars."

In his speech asking Congress for a Declaration of War, Woodrow Wilson proclaimed: "The world must be made safe for democracy. . . . [There must be] a universal dominion of right by such a concert of free peoples as shall bring peace and safety to all nations and make the world itself at last free."[5]

This idealism of America was captured best by four words spoken by the first American troops arriving in France. On July 4th, they marched through Paris to the Tomb of Lafayette and said: "Lafayette, we are here!"[6]

HAKUNA MATATA

The Great War became the "Great Nightmare." American soldiers in France soon discovered the horror of living in trenches, enduring artillery bombardments, and dying in gas attacks.

When the War was over, Americans wanted nothing more than to return home and live happily ever after. I best learned this from my Grandma and Grandpa Harner. (Grandpa Harner served in France during World War I.) When they were quite elderly (about 1970), I asked them why they didn't worry about what would happen to Europe after World War I. They didn't seem to grasp my question: "Why didn't America join the League of Nations after the War?"

When I pressed them for their memories of that distant time, they said, "We didn't know anything about that. We just wanted to get married. People said it was the first time that the country was without a President."

People complained that "the country was without a President" because Woodrow Wilson sailed to Europe for the Peace Conference. Wilson was seeking a peace that would justify all of the death and suffering. He was still pursuing his idealistic crusade to make the world safe for democracy and to end all wars.

In Europe, he received a harsh dose of reality. France and Britain were in no mood for a peace crafted "with malice toward none and with charity for all." France wanted revenge for the rape of her land by the "Huns." France also wanted to weaken Germany so that France could live happily ever after. Britain wanted money and colonies from Germany. Everybody wanted Germany to admit that Germany was guilty for starting the war.

Despite so much hatred, Wilson won agreement on establishing his greatest dream: a League of Nations. As he had promised when America declared war, there would be "a universal dominion of right by such a concert of free peoples as shall bring peace and safety to all nations and make the world itself at last free."

Unfortunately, back home in the United States, he received another harsh dose of reality. Most Americans were tired of making the world safe for democracy. As disillusionment set in about the war, people felt a renewed admiration for the wisdom of George Washington, who'd warned, in his Farewell Address: "'Tis our true policy to steer clear of permanent alliances with any portion of the foreign world."

The American people were deceiving themselves. In their fervent desire *not* to go to war, they were not seeing the changes in the world, they were not hearing the changes in the world, and they were not understanding the changes in the world.

At the time that George Washington gave his Farewell Address, it took weeks to cross the Atlantic in sailing ships. Now mighty vessels traversed the Atlantic in a few days. Soon Charles Lindbergh would cross the Atlantic in an airplane.

When George Washington gave his Farewell Address, the United States was a nation of farmers. Now the United States was the greatest industrial power in the world.

Woodrow Wilson ruined his health and shortened his life crisscrossing America trying to build support for joining the League of Nations. Still, he failed. The Republicans regained control of the White House, pursuing policies that kept America prosperous until the Great Depression and that kept America at peace until Pearl Harbor. Obviously, *popular* policies are not always *wise* policies.

A good way to describe the mood of America during these years of peace and prosperity is to call it "Hakuna Matata." The Disney classic, *The Lion King*, made the phrase Hakuna Matata famous. Simba (a lion cub who was supposed to become king) ran away from his problems instead of facing them. His new friends, Pumba (a warthog) and Timon (a meerkat), taught him to live in the carefree manner that they called Hakuna Matata: a "problem-free philosophy" that "means no worries for the rest of your days."[1]

Such shirking of responsibilities is fun for awhile, but in real life—as in *The Lion King*—Hakuna Matata ends in disaster. Back home in the Pridelands, Simba's people suffered poverty under the foolish rule of his Uncle Scar. In the real world, people in America and around the world suffered poverty because of the foolish policies of tight money and high tariffs that caused the Great Depression. The Great Depression lingered because the nations of the world—and especially America—preferred to go their separate ways instead of banding together to solve global economic problems.

Back home in the Pridelands, Simba's Uncle Scarface was a tyrant who oppressed Simba's people. In the real world, people suffered and died under tyrants such as Hitler and Stalin while America looked the other way.

Back home in the Pridelands, Simba's Uncle Scar was a bully who allied himself with the hyenas. In the real world, bullies such as Hitler and Imperial Japan plotted war while America looked the other way.

In *The Lion King*, Simba finally accepted his responsibilities and made things right after his dead father urged him in a vision: *"Remember! Remember who you are!!!"* In the real world, President Franklin Roosevelt reminded Americans who we are. He reminded Americans that the Torch of Liberty still shines in our hearts—and liberty is never without sacrifice.

By the time Roosevelt died after twelve years in office, the Torch of Liberty was shining across the world. America was making the world safe for democracy. And America was founding the United Nations to fulfill Woodrow Wilson's vision of "a universal dominion of right by such a concert of free peoples as shall bring peace and safety to all nations and make the world itself at last free."

Such was the vision of Franklin Roosevelt for America.

In the midst of the Great Depression, Roosevelt defied despair with his maxim: "There is nothing to fear but fear itself." In his personal life, Roosevelt overcame the paralysis of polio (even though its effects plagued him for the rest of his life). And by mobilizing America to fight the Great Depression . . . just as America had been mobilized to fight the Great War, Roosevelt overcame the national paralysis of the Great Depression (even though its effects plagued America for the rest of the 1930s).

Unfortunately, not even the popularity and wisdom of Franklin D. Roosevelt could convince America to confront Hitler until it was almost too late. In 1940, France fell to Nazi tanks and dive-bombers. Britain, led by the indomitable Winston Churchill, fought bravely on. But despite Britain's heroic struggle against hopeless odds, the triumphant Nazi war machine appeared invincible.

In January 1941, as London burned beneath nightly bombing raids, Franklin Roosevelt set forth his vision for the future of America and for all Humanity:

> In the future days, which we seek to make secure, we look forward to a world founded upon four essential human freedoms. The first is freedom of speech and expression—everywhere in the world. The second is freedom of every person to worship God in his own way—everywhere in the world. The third is freedom from want . . . everywhere in the world. The fourth is freedom from fear . . . *anywhere* in the world.

As his vision for America and the world shows, Roosevelt saw that liberty is never safe anywhere in the world until liberty is safe *every*where in the world. He saw and heard the world shrinking as planes now circled the globe and as radio reached every home.

Roosevelt understood that liberty and union (with all other free peoples) are one and inseparable. And so, in 1941, Franklin Roosevelt and Winston Churchill took a gigantic step toward establishing a universal dominion of right by a concert of free peoples to bring peace and safety to all nations and to make the world itself at last free. A few months before the Japanese sneak attack on Pearl Harbor that drew America into World War II, Franklin Roosevelt and Winston Churchill issued the Atlantic Charter. On behalf of the English-speaking peoples, they proclaimed that:

[A]fter the final destruction of the Nazi tyranny, they hope to see established a peace which will afford to all nations the means of dwelling in safety within their boundaries, and which will afford assurance that all the men in all the lands may live out their lives in freedom from fear and want.

The English-speaking peoples were preparing to come in peace for all Humanity.

RAISING THE STAR-SPANGLED BANNER

Before we could come in peace for all Humanity, many struggles lay ahead. The first struggle was "the final destruction of the Nazi tyranny."[1]

The essence of this struggle is captured best by the Marine Corps Memorial in Washington, D.C.—that famous statue of American troops raising the Star-Spangled Banner in victory at Iwo Jima. The actual battle depicted by the statue was fought against Japan, not against Germany. But the struggle against Japan was part of the struggle against Hitler, the evil demon who preached that his race was superior to all other races, who deliberately started World War II, who brainstormed and led the Holocaust, and who gloried in his gruesome mission of genocide.

The toil and triumph of battle are carved in the forms and etched in the faces of these victorious Americans. The Star-Spangled Banner waves majestically in the breeze as the Americans strain to plant it firmly in the earth.

For me, the most meaningful inspiration that comes from gazing at the statue is a realization that Americans have only just begun to raise their Star-Spangled Banner. It is rising towards the heavens, even though it is not yet firmly planted in the earth.

A battle is won. But the war is far from over:

- The War against all who are racists.
- The War against all who start wars.
- The War against all who persecute others.

• The War against all who love to hate.

America has come far. But America has much further to go. In fact, we've only just begun.[2]

THE BUCK STOPS HERE

President Truman is best remembered for his colorful statement that "The Buck Stops Here." That phrase captured Truman's determination to do his best and to leave the rest, confident that it will all come out right some day or night.[1]

This mood filled America as World War II ended. Having become convinced that a key reason for the Great Depression and World War II was that America had not acted responsibly after World War I, Americans were determined to do better this time.

And so, under President Truman, America took an active role in establishing global prosperity through The Marshall Plan to help rebuild the wartime devastation in Europe. America realized that the German people and the Japanese people had been deceived and manipulated by a few evil leaders. Accordingly, peace was reached with Germany and Japan based on Abraham Lincoln's wisdom after our Civil War: "with malice toward none and with charity for all."

America also saw that there were still evil aggressors in the world who must be confronted. Therefore, when Stalin tried to snuff out freedom in West Berlin, Truman organized the Berlin Airlift to keep the Torch of Liberty shining in Europe. When the North Koreans (with the help of the Chinese) invaded South Korea, Truman sent American troops to keep the Torch of Liberty shining in Asia.

Truman was also wise enough to realize that, because of the atomic bomb, the world was changing. Although he was willing to drop atomic bombs on the Japanese cities of Hiroshima and Nagasaki in order to bring a quick end to World War II, Truman realized that a third world war would bring an end to all civilization, and perhaps to all Humanity.

PART I: Peace for All Humanity

Therefore, in Europe and Asia, Truman was willing to *contain* Russian and Chinese aggression, but he refused to allow flamboyant, popular World War II generals such as Patton and MacArthur to lure America into a war to *destroy* Communism.

Instead of using bombs to *destroy* America's enemies, Truman decided to give the Torch of Liberty enough time to *convert* America's enemies.

Truman was patient. Truman was wise. And Truman was right.

THE NEW FRONTIER

By 1960, it looked far more as if the Communists would destroy the Torch of Liberty than that the Torch of Liberty would destroy the Communists.

The first fifteen years after World War II marked a string of victories for the Communists. The eastern half of Europe lay behind the "Iron Curtain," kept firmly under the domination of the Soviet Union. The "Soviet fist" was dramatically illustrated in Hungary in 1956. A revolt in Hungary's capital, Budapest, briefly tossed out the Communist puppets of the Soviet Union. But the leader of the Soviet Union, Nikita Khrushchev, sent tanks rolling into Hungary, brutally re-establishing Communist tyranny.

In Asia, the immense population of Red China was taught to hate America. In the Korean War, the United States learned the horror of fighting innumerable hoards of fanatically dedicated Chinese troops. Japan, South Korea, and Taiwan remained within United States control, but at that time these countries were economically backward. When I was growing up, things that were "Made in Japan" were cheap, shoddy items such as souvenirs at tourist traps. Today, Japanese imports to America include the finest in technological tools, automobiles, and electronics.

The Communists took advantage of the turmoil in Southern Asia, the Middle East, and Africa. In these immense regions with burgeoning populations and vast natural resources, colonialism was coming to an end. European allies of the United States such as

Britain and France were losing their colonies. Nationalistic movements in these countries often turned to the Soviet Union for help.

The refusal of non-Europeans to submit to rule by whites globally was mirrored by the refusal of African-Americans to continue submitting to segregation in America. In 1954, the United States Supreme Court ruled that states could no longer have separate schools for whites and blacks. For the next decade, court-ordered integration of educational institutions sent shock waves of fear and violence throughout the South. For the first time since the Compromise of 1876, the Federal government intervened in the South to protect the civil rights of black people.

In 1955, in Montgomery, Alabama, a black woman named Rosa Parks refused to move to a seat in the back of a city bus so that a white person could take her seat at the front of the bus. When Rosa Parks was arrested for breaking the law that required segregation on the buses, the African-American community refused to ride the buses until segregation ended. The Rev. Martin Luther King, Jr., a young African-American preacher at a Montgomery Baptist church, became their legendary leader.

As the United States faced fearsome enemies abroad and turmoil at home, paranoia ruled the day. Some Americans—most notably United States Senator Joe McCarthy—believed that Communist spies and sympathizers were everywhere. Political hearings with all the earmarks of "witchhunts" were conducted publicly, smearing loyal Americans for their beliefs, their affiliations, or for their "unfortunate," politically incorrect choice of friends.

Some Americans—most notably the Director of the FBI, J. Edgar Hoover—believed that Communists were instigating the entire Civil Rights movement in an effort to weaken the United States from within. In an atmosphere of racist paranoia, some couldn't seem to imagine that loyal African-Americans simply wanted a good education for their children and the same right to life, liberty, and the pursuit of happiness that other Americans enjoyed.

Fear permeated the social milieu. It seemed as if the only hope of staving off "the innumerable hoards of Communists" in Russia and China was to fortify the technological supremacy of the United States. But in 1957, American faith in its own technological supremacy crumbled. The Soviet Union succeeded in sending the first satellite, called "Sputnik," into orbit in outer space. The desperate efforts of the United States to match this demonstration of Communist supremacy ended in humiliating failures. For example, an American rocket exploded on the launch pad in full view of a worldwide television audience. (The Russians only publicized their successes. Their failures were kept top secret.)

In addition to this blow to United States pride and prestige from Sputnik, there was a more sinister edge to the Soviet's triumphs in space. The same rockets that could launch satellites could also launch nuclear weapons. Obviously, the Soviet missiles would be much better at destroying *our* cities than our missiles would be at destroying *their* cities.

As the humiliation of losing the "space race" sank in, another humiliation struck home. Cuba fell to the Communists. In 1959, Fidel Castro, with his infamous beard and jaunty cigar, overthrew a government that was friendly towards the United States, then quickly allied himself with the Soviet Union and Red China. From his outpost off the coast of Florida, the Communists threatened to topple governments throughout the Western Hemisphere.

For 150 years, the linchpin of United States security had been the Monroe Doctrine. No European nation was allowed to establish colonies, or otherwise intervene in, the Western Hemisphere. This meant that no European enemy of the United States would have bases in the Western Hemisphere from which to attack it.

Suddenly, the security of living safely sheltered from invasion by the immense waters of the Atlantic and Pacific Oceans was stripped away. Not only could nuclear missiles launched from Russia swoop down on our cities with only about 20 minutes' warning. Now the Communists could easily launch internal subversion and guerrilla wars from Cuban bases against the United States and her allies throughout the Western Hemisphere.

Faced with these dire perils, Americans had to choose between Richard Nixon and John Fitzgerald Kennedy in the 1960 Presidential election. Nixon had served as Vice President for the past eight years under President Eisenhower, the popular (but aging) World War II General who led the Allied invasion of Europe. Nixon was experienced in foreign policy and was also a tough-minded politician. Kennedy had very little government experience, but he had youth, charm, and personal charisma. For the first time in history, Americans viewed these two presidential candidates in publicly televised debates.

In a very close election, Kennedy edged out Nixon. Americans decided that it was time for a change–for vigorous new leadership that would revive American efforts to match the dynamic Communist challenge around the globe.

Kennedy spoke passionately about his vision of America—his vision of a New Frontier. During the Presidential campaign, Kennedy explained that he wanted to lead America to this New Frontier. He said, "The New Frontier of which I speak is not a set of promises—it is a set of challenges."[1]

In his Inaugural Address, Kennedy laid these challenges before the American people and all Humanity. Speaking as the first President from the generation of Americans who'd endured the Great Depression and won the Second World War, Kennedy said:

> Let the word go forth from this time and place, to friend and foe alike, that the torch has been passed to a new generation of Americans, born in this century, tempered by war, disciplined by a hard and bitter peace, proud of our ancient heritage, and unwilling to witness or permit the slow undoing of those human rights to which this nation has always been committed. . . .

> Let every nation know, whether it wishes us well or ill, that we shall pay any price, bear any burden, meet any hardship, support any friend, oppose any foe to assure the survival and the success of liberty. . . .

> [T]he trumpet summons us . . . to bear the burden of a long twilight struggle, year in and year out, "rejoicing in hope, patient in tribulation," a struggle against the common enemies of

man: tyranny, poverty, disease and war itself. . . . The energy, the faith, the devotion which we bring to this endeavor will light our country and all who serve it, and the glow from that fire can truly light the world.

The glow of the Torch of Liberty never shone brighter than when President Kennedy led America against the common enemies of Humanity: tyranny, poverty, disease and war itself.

That is why the Thousand Days during which President Kennedy led America are remembered as "Camelot"—a time when the courage and wisdom of America's "King Arthur" led us through "The Valley of the Shadow of the Death" of all Humanity in a nuclear holocaust.

The Cuban Missile Crisis

For thirteen days in 1962, Humanity teetered on the brink of destruction, almost committing suicide with nuclear weapons. We call those days "The Cuban Missile Crisis."

In fact, there had been a perpetual series of crises ever since World War II ended, starting with Truman's willingness to airlift supplies to West Berlin to keep it free. But no crisis ever came closer to destroying all Humanity than the crisis that erupted in October, 1962, over the nuclear missiles that the Soviet Union located in Cuba.

It was bad enough that the Soviet Union dared to flaunt its defiance of the Monroe Doctrine that marked America's determination to keep foreign military threats out of the Western Hemisphere. What made it worse was that Nikita Khrushchev blatantly lied about his intentions in Cuba. Publicly and privately, the Communists had given repeated, definitive promises that they would not put nuclear missiles in Cuba.[1]

Khrushchev must have hoped that he could secretly install his nuclear missiles on the island before the United States discovered what he was up to. He underestimated the close watch that U.S. spy planes kept on Cuba. Fortunately, the United States obtained aerial photos of the missiles when they were being installed—*before* they became operational.

Khrushchev also underestimated how infuriated the United States would be when the missiles were discovered. From Khrushchev's perspective (and with some historical justification), the United States had been bullying Cuba and other Latin American countries for a century. Indeed, as recently as 1961 (a few months after Kennedy took office) the United States had once again displayed its imperialist instincts: the CIA backed an unsuccessful invasion of Cuba at the Bay of Pigs in order to try and overthrow Castro.

Why shouldn't Cuba be free to pursue its own economic and political agenda, even if the United States didn't like it? Furthermore, if the United States didn't like Soviet nuclear missiles near its coast, why did the United States think that it should continue to have nuclear missiles in Turkey along the border of the Soviet Union?

But the United States saw only that it faced a deceitful foe as bent on world tyranny and domination as Adolf Hitler. Giving in to Hitler had only encouraged him to make more threats and conquests. Therefore, the United States was intransigent: *the missiles must go!*

Many of President Kennedy's advisors urged him to take direct military action to destroy the missiles before they became operational. This would mean air strikes and, in all likelihood, an invasion.

However, Kennedy had recently read *The Guns of August*, Barbara Tuchman's classic account describing how the Europeans foolishly stumbled into World War I. Kennedy was determined that no one would ever write a book about how he had foolishly stumbled into World War III![2]

Kennedy wisely decided to show restraint as well as firmness. Instead of ordering air strikes or an invasion, Kennedy ordered the U.S. Navy to stop any ships carrying offensive military equipment to Cuba.

The President's brother, Bobby Kennedy, later wrote about the climactic moment when Soviet cargo ships arrived at the spot where United States ships were going to stop them. A Soviet submarine was in position between the cargo ships.

Would the Soviet ships sail on, forcing the United States to fire the first shot? Would the Soviet submarine fire the first shot? Or would the Soviet ships stop?

Bobby Kennedy recalled what it was like to wait for the news of whether war had begun:

> I think these few minutes were the time of gravest concern for the President. Was the world on the brink of a holocaust? Was it our error? A mistake? . . . His hand went up to his face and covered his mouth. He opened and closed his fist. His face seemed drawn, his eyes pained, almost gray.[3]

At last, word came that the Soviet ships had stopped and were turning around. Bobby Kennedy remembered the relief that flooded the room: "[E]veryone looked like a different person. For a moment the world had stood still, and now it was going around again."[4]

Eventually, a face-saving compromise was reached that resolved the crisis. The United States promised not to invade Cuba, the Soviets pulled their nuclear missiles out of Cuba, and the United States removed its nuclear missiles from Turkey.

The Cold War continued for almost thirty more years. But after this moment of mutual terror, the Cold War began to thaw. Never again did the Soviet Union and the United States come to the brink of a nuclear holocaust. There would now be time for the Torch of Liberty to convert the Communists to a way of life that ensures everyone's rights of life, liberty, and the pursuit of happiness.

THE ASSASSINATION OF PRESIDENT KENNEDY

Historians will no doubt underestimate the impact of President Kennedy on history.

They never lived through the stress of the Cuban Missile Crisis. Reading the historical records, they already *know* that a nuclear holocaust was averted.

Furthermore, most "armchair historians" of today never lived through the trauma of the assassination of President Kennedy on November 22, 1963. They never experienced the national pain and grief of those days.

John F. Kennedy is not only important because he could have destroyed Humanity by making a mistake during the Cuban Missile Crisis. Kennedy is important because his sudden, violent death, galvanized America into action.

Just as a child sometimes becomes a compulsive overachiever to fulfill the dreams of a dead mother or father, Americans became compulsive overachievers during the 1960s to fulfill the dreams of their beloved, slain "King Arthur." And just as being an overachiever can both help and hurt a child, America's desperate efforts to fulfill Kennedy's dreams both helped and hurt America.

In South Vietnam, the United States fought doggedly to stop the spread of Communism. But for a variety of reasons, this effort to contain Communism failed. Instead of seeing, hearing, and understanding that battling Communism in this place and in this way was futile, America desperately tried to keep faith with Kennedy's promise in his Inaugural Address that we would "pay any price, bear any burden, meet any hardship, support any friend, oppose any foe, to assure the survival and the success of liberty." Hence, more and more American young people were sent to Vietnam. Billions of dollars were wasted that could have been spent on a far more important war: the War on Poverty.

The vision of President Lyndon B. Johnson for America was that his "Great Society" would win a War on Poverty. Johnson entered politics with the motivation to fight the Great Depression as a staunch supporter of President Roosevelt's New Deal. In Congress, Johnson was a brilliant legislative leader, and he eventually became the Senate Majority Leader. Johnson left the Senate to become Kennedy's Vice President. When Kennedy was assassinated, Johnson became the President.

Using the legislative skills that he'd learned as the Senate Majority Leader and capitalizing on America's yearning to fulfill Kennedy's dreams, President Johnson passed law after law that expanded Roosevelt's "New Deal" into a "Great Society" and a "War on Poverty."

In large measure, the War on Poverty and the quest for the Great Society were disastrous failures. Indeed, a basic flaw in Johnson's leadership skills was responsible for America's defeat in the War on Poverty, as well as for America's defeat in the Vietnam War.

As a legislative leader, Johnson was brilliant at compromising and at passing laws. But as President, he lacked the originality and flexibility needed to achieve his goals. For example, Johnson knew that his hero, President Roosevelt, had failed to contain Hitler's aggression before Hitler became so powerful that a world war became inevitable. Johnson had seen the "domino effect" that giving in to aggression brings. One success encourages the aggressor to seek more ill gotten gains. The next time, the aggressor is even more powerful because his strength is increased by his exploitation of the conquered territories. Meanwhile, the strength of those opposing the aggressor is decreased by the loss of the conquered territories.

After World War II, Johnson had seen how quickly the Communists had gobbled up the eastern half of Europe and all of Red China. Truman stopped this "domino effect" in Europe by risking nuclear war and stopped the "domino effect" in Asia by fighting a war in Korea that ended in a bloody stalemate.

Johnson had seen how Kennedy had forced the Communists to remove missiles from Cuba even though it meant risking nuclear war. Therefore, Johnson blindly followed similar approaches to stopping the spread of Communism in Southeast Asia. Fearful of the "domino effect" if South Vietnam fell to the Communists, Johnson was willing to keep fighting in Vietnam indefinitely in a bloody stalemate.

Johnson was blind to the changes in the world. He was unable to see, hear, and understand ways to change the military and diplomatic conditions that were inflicting this defeat on America. Johnson just kept wasting more and more money—and more and more lives—in a futile struggle. Privately, President Johnson may have agonized over the many lives being lost in Vietnam. But publicly, Johnson appeared unable to see, hear, or understand the horrors of war.

Truman was a wise "physician" for America. To save the life of a "Free World" that was "bleeding to death" by losing country after country to the Communists after World War II, Truman wisely applied a tourniquet to stop the bleeding.

After the Cuban Missile Crisis awakened both America and the Soviet Union to the genuine peril of nuclear annihilation, the Cold War began to thaw. The time had come to seek peace "with malice toward none and with charity for all." The time had come to loosen the tourniquet before lack of "blood" caused gangrene and the world itself died.

Johnson did not see, hear, or understand this. He tightened the tourniquet, ignoring the fact that he was killing the patient that he thought he was helping. Thus the War in Vietnam became a battle in the Cold War that can only be compared in its stupidity to the battle of Fredericksburg in the Civil War.

As you may recall, the Union defeat at Fredericksburg resulted from the best of intentions. The Union commander, General Burnside, knew that President Lincoln wanted him to fight Robert E. Lee and that President Lincoln wanted him to capture Richmond. So Burnside marched straight toward Richmond and attacked Lee's army where he found it—across a river in a fortified position on top of a hill.

With incredible stupidity, Burnside did not try to march someplace else for a battle. Instead, with criminal foolishness, Burnside simply ordered his troops to cross the river and attack up the hill. Of course, his troops were slaughtered. And the bloody disaster could easily have led to a victory for the Confederacy in the Civil War.

In short, at the battle of Fredericksburg the noble sacrifice and indomitable courage of the Union soldiers were surpassed only by the incredible stupidity and criminal foolishness of their leaders. Similarly, in Vietnam, the noble sacrifice and indomitable courage of the soldiers who fought for a democratic, free South Vietnam was surpassed only by the incredible stupidity and criminal foolishness of their leaders. And the bloody disaster could easily have led to a victory for the Communists in the Cold War.

In his futile quest for a Great Society that would win the War on Poverty, Johnson displayed the same lack of originality—the same inability to "think outside the box"—that led to the military disaster in Vietnam.

Johnson knew that, during the Great Depression, his hero, President Roosevelt, saved America from the Great Depression by creating massive government programs to help people and to jumpstart the economy. He blindly assumed that, during the 1960s, massive government programs were the best way—and the *only* way—to help people and to reinvigorate the economy.

Once again, President Johnson did not see, hear, or understand the sweeping social changes at work in the world of his time. Johnson just kept wasting more and more money in a futile War on Poverty and in a futile quest for a Great Society.

Johnson was unable to see, hear, or understand that Roosevelt had been America's "physician" at a time when her economy was broken. In that crisis, Roosevelt wisely used the full powers of government to treat the ailing patient by putting casts on her broken limbs and giving her drugs for her pain.

In the 1960s, the economy was strong. To overcome the sluggish economic growth of the 1950s, Kennedy stimulated the economy with tax cuts and stressed good education to assure America's long-term prosperity. A wise physician, Kennedy knew that the best way for his patient, America, to get stronger was to remove the casts on her limbs so that she could exercise her muscles and to stop giving her drugs so that she could exercise her mind. Kennedy motivated the patient by challenging her to explore New Frontiers . . . such as going to the moon and overcoming "the common enemies of man: tyranny, poverty, disease, and war itself."

President Johnson inflicted serious wounds on America, put her into a body cast of government regulation, and drugged America so badly that she lost her vision. Wasting money at home and in Vietnam created an overheated, over-regulated economy that prospered in the 1960s, then nearly collapsed in the 1970s.

The combination of military disaster in Vietnam and economic disaster at home nearly led to America losing the Cold War. Ironically, the one bright spot of the 1960s was also the result of America funneling more and more money into a government program. In this case, America achieved something totally new: America sent men to the moon.

Unfortunately, even in this grand adventure—comparable to Christopher Columbus reaching America in 1492—America was content to stop once Kennedy's vision was fulfilled. America sent men to the moon, but failed to take the next logical steps: a space station, putting tourists in space, scientists on the moon, and settlers on Mars.

In the disasters that struck America due to President Johnson's blunders, America lost the vision to boldly go where no one had gone before. And she almost lost the vision of the Torch of Liberty that alone could win victory in the Cold War.

The Bible warns us that "[w]here there is no vision, the people perish" (Proverbs 29:18, KJV). In 1963, an assassin struck down a visionary leader of America: President Kennedy. As a result, America almost perished.

THE ASSASSINATION OF MARTIN LUTHER KING

Many reasons are given for the success of the Civil Rights Movement of the 1950s and 1960s. Certainly, television was important. For the first time, all Americans could see firsthand the ugly face of segregation in the South.

World War II and the Holocaust were also essential ingredients in changing people's attitudes toward racism and prejudice. Hitler launched World War II in the belief that he led the "Master Race" and declared that the world would be a better place if "inferior" peoples, such as the Jews, were exterminated and if "flawed" peoples, such as the mentally infirm and homosexual, were exterminated, too. The resulting horror of the Holocaust enabled everyone to see, hear, and understand that such hatred is evil.

Fortunately, nothing keeps the Torch of Liberty shining more brightly than the courage and vision of people who know that we can overcome hatred, injustice, and prejudice. Hence, just as George Washington's vision of America was indispensable to victory in the War for Independence and Abraham Lincoln's vision of America was indispensable to victory in the Civil War, Martin Luther King's vision of America was indispensable to victory in the Civil Rights Movement.

Indeed, Martin Luther King's vision of America became indispensable to victory in the Cold War. His vision allowed us to hope that people could overcome tyranny through nonviolent but direct action—without annihilating all Humanity in a "Third World War." The threat of universal extinction from nuclear weapons gave rise to a moral imperative toward nonviolence that had, apart from Mahatma Ghandi's valiant struggle for independence in colonial India, not heretofore been present in human history.

And so, instead of telling blacks to kill whites in revenge for centuries of enslavement and exploitation, Martin Luther King found the faith to hope that whites could change. He wanted to *convert* whites to his vision of America, not *destroy* them.

This vision of an America glowing in the light of the Torch of Liberty is enshrined in the speech that Martin Luther King delivered from the top of the steps of the Lincoln Memorial during the historic March on Washington in August, 1963. Although no one knew or could have imagined it on this day, President Kennedy would be slain in only a few months.

We've all seen videos of the inspiring moment. As Martin Luther King stands at the microphone, he sees a sea of white and black faces stretching across the Mall with its reflecting pool, the spire of Washington's Monument, and the distant dome of the Capitol.

A few months later, Martin Luther King described what happened this way. He started reading from his prepared speech. But then, "just all of a sudden—the audience response was wonderful that day—and all of a sudden this thing came to me that I have used—I'd used it many times before, that thing about 'I have a dream'—and I just felt that I wanted to use it here. I don't know why, I hadn't thought about it before the speech."[1]

How can we doubt that the Spirit of God inspired Martin Luther King that day?

How can we doubt that the Spirit of God gave him the dream that would move America and change all Humanity?

The Spirit of God enabled him to dream of the America that Abraham saw when he left behind his homeland to seek a land where all people would be blessed. The Spirit of God enabled him to dream of the America that Moses saw when he told Pharaoh to let his people go free.

The Spirit of God enabled him to dream of the America that Jesus saw when he taught us to be Good Samaritans who will bind the wounds of those in need even though we have been taught to hate them because of their race, their nation, or their religion.

The Spirit of God gave Martin Luther King these words whose fruit is love, joy, peace, patience, kindness, goodness, faithfulness, gentleness, and self-control (Galatians 5:22–23):

> I . . . have a dream. It is a dream deeply rooted in the American dream. I have a dream that one day this nation will rise up and live out the true meaning of its creed—we hold these truths to be self-evident, that all men are created equal.

> I have a dream that one day . . . the sons of former slaves and the sons of former slave-owners will be able to sit down together at the table of brotherhood. . . .

> I have a dream that my four little children will one day live in a nation where they will not be judged by the color of their skin but by the content of their character. I have a dream today!

> I have a dream that one day . . . little black boys and black girls will be able to join hands with little white boys and white girls as sisters and brothers. I have a dream today!

I have a dream that one day every valley shall be exalted, every hill and mountain shall be made low, the rough places will be made plain, and the crooked places will be made straight and the glory of the Lord shall be revealed and all flesh shall see it together.

The crowd grew louder and louder as each person in it dreamed Martin Luther King's dream, as each person saw Martin Luther King's vision of America. In his vision, we "let freedom ring" from every mountainside in the East, from every mountain peak in the West, and from every valley in the South. Because:

When we allow freedom to ring, when we let it ring from every village and every hamlet, from every state and every city, we will be able to speed up that day when all of God's children—black men and white men, Jews and Gentiles, Protestants and Catholics—will be able to join hands and sing in the words of the old Negro spiritual, 'Free at last, free at last; thank God Almighty, we are free at last.'[2]

As the years passed, Martin Luther King's dream turned, for the time being, into nightmares.

The North supported his challenge to the practice of segregation in the South (where segregation was enforced by law). But Northerners developed a "white backlash" when he challenged segregation in the North (where segregation was enforced by social pressure).

Anger grew against Martin Luther King's dream when he challenged the economic exploitation of both blacks *and* whites in America. Even more outrage flared when Martin Luther King outspokenly challenged the immorality of the war in Vietnam.

Many powerful people—including, most notably, J. Edgar Hoover, the head of the FBI—had long feared that Martin Luther King was being used by the Communists to weaken the United States from within. As race riots mounted, and as Martin Luther King expanded his "agenda" to include economic and foreign policy issues, such paranoid people saw their worst fears being confirmed.

Perhaps for these reasons there has long been suspicion that conspirators who were somehow connected, directly or indirectly, with the Federal government, played some role in the assassination of Martin Luther King. No proof has been found, but because of the anger and fear that Martin Luther King's dreams caused, suspicion still lingers.

Martin Luther King was an inspirational leader, but was not a perfect man—far from it. For example, in order to blackmail King, the FBI tape-recorded his adulterous escapades.

The Old Testament hero, Samson, also fell into immorality. Nevertheless, God used Samson to begin to set his people free from the Philistines (Judges 13:5). Furthermore, Samson is listed in the Bible amongst the greatest heroes of the faith (Hebrews 11:32). And although Samson was weakened and blinded by his sins, God gave Samson one last burst of strength as he died. Indeed, in his dying act, Samson did more to set his people free than he had ever done in his lifetime (Judges 16:30).

In the months before his assassination, Martin Luther King grew discouraged and weary. Like Samson, his discouragement stemmed, in part, from his inability to control his own sexual immorality. But—also like Samson of old—God gave him one last burst of strength to set his people free by overcoming their foes: tyranny, poverty, disease, and war itself.

It was the night before his death. An exhausted Martin Luther King rested wearily in his hotel room in Memphis. A crowd of two thousand people was gathering for the rally that night. Discouragement grew when they were told that King himself would not be coming. At the last moment, a phone call was made, urging King to change his mind and come. As always, Martin Luther King answered the call to come and give hope to the people.

Rain and wind battered the building. Windows rattled. Because there had been a bomb threat on the plane he'd taken that day, the possibility of dying was on Martin Luther King's mind that stormy night. As before, when he had fallen into morbid moods, he thought about Moses (who died before he could enter the Promised Land), beholding the Promised Land from a mountaintop just before he died. And so, Martin Luther King ended his ministry with these "last words" that were played over and over again after his death the next day:

> Well, I don't know what will happen now. We've got some difficult days ahead. But it really doesn't matter with me now, because I've been to the mountaintop. And I don't mind. Like anybody, I would like to live a long life. Longevity has its place. But I'm not concerned about that now. I just want to do God's will. And He's allowed me to go up to the mountain, and I've looked over, and I've seen the Promised Land. I may not get there with you. But I want you to know tonight, that we, as a people will get to the Promised Land. And so I'm happy tonight. I'm not worried about anything. I'm not fearing any man. Mine eyes have seen the glory of the coming of the Lord.[3]

I think that—in the aftermath of his death the next day—these last words from Martin Luther King touched white America more deeply than any of his previous speeches. Therefore, in his death, Martin Luther King did more to set his people free than he had ever done in his lifetime.

By way of personal example, in our white Baptist church, the pastor had never before spoken about the Civil Rights Movement. Yet on that Sunday after Martin Luther King was martyred because "[he] just want[ed] to do God's will," our pastor praised "Brother Martin"—a fellow Baptist preacher who was now in heaven, having seen the Promised Land and having seen the Glory of the Coming of the Lord.

In the long run, Martin Luther King's vision of America prevailed. But in the short run, hatred prevailed. Riots burned American cities. African-Americans despaired. White Americans worried, "What's gone wrong with America?"

The Bible warns us that "[w]here there is no vision, the people perish" (Proverbs 29:18, KJV).

In 1968, an assassin struck down a visionary leader of America: Martin Luther King. And as a result, America almost perished.

THE ASSASSINATION OF BOBBY KENNEDY

When Martin Luther King died, the major cities of America erupted in race riots. Eventually, the flames burned themselves out, leaving smoldering anger amidst the ashes of despair.

Meanwhile, in Vietnam, the killing went on. The trust of the American people in their government was severely shaken by the "Tet Offensive" that the Communists had launched in January, 1968.

Prior to the Tet Offensive, the United States military claimed that the Communists were losing the Vietnam War. But in the Tet Offensive, the Communists launched massive attacks that inflicted heavy casualties on United States troops. Therefore, it became obvious that the United States was either being led by fools, who had not realized how powerful the Communists actually were, or by liars, who did not want the American people to *know* how powerful the Communists actually were.

Under these circumstances, many people in the Democratic Party began to have severe doubts about re-nominating the inept President Lyndon B. Johnson for another term. Johnson was almost beaten in the Democratic Primary in New Hampshire by the previously unknown Democratic Senator Eugene McCarthy. Soon afterwards, Johnson announced that he would not run for re-election.

Bobby Kennedy ran for President on the Democratic ticket, conjuring up memories of the New Frontiers that once beckoned a happier America. With a charming Boston accent that reminded people of his slain brother, Bobby Kennedy inspired people with his own political vision of America: "Some men see things as they are, and say, 'Why?' I dream of things that never were, and say, 'Why not?'"[1]

Like many public figures, Kennedy was outspoken—and was both loved and hated by many. People fretted that "some nut" would kill Bobby, as they had Jack Kennedy. To the country's horror, in his moment of victory in the California Primary, the feared scenario became a grim reality. As people celebrated his victory, a man with a gun got close enough to shoot Bobby Kennedy in the head.

Bobby lingered for a day. I remember going to school the morning after he'd been shot. We weren't allowed to pray in school. Instead, they told us all to go outside the school, circle the flagpole, and have a "moment of silence" in the hope that a miracle might yet save Bobby.

The next morning, Bobby was dead. Once again, we all circled the flagpole to have a "moment of silence" in memory of Bobby Kennedy and in the hope that a miracle might yet save America.

The Bible warns us that "[w]here there is no vision, the people perish" (Proverbs 29:18, KJV).

On the fifth of June 1968, an assassin struck down another visionary leader of America: Bobby Kennedy. And as a result, America almost perished.

Apollo 8

Many reasons are given for the success of the Environmental Movement in the 1970s. Certainly, television was important. For the first time, all Americans could see the ugly face of pollution.

However, the picture that I believe most encouraged the Environmental Movement was not a picture of the ugliness of pollution. It was a picture of the beauty of the earth. It was a picture that the spacecraft Apollo 8 took, on Christmas Eve in 1968, of the earth rising over the rim of the moon.

The earth looked so vulnerable. So precious . . . nothing but a fragile blue and white oasis hanging alone in the darkness.

The lifeless, dusty pallor of the moon accentuated the lively, colorful glow of the earth. This new perspective on the earth, Humanity, and God inspired the reading of Scripture by the Apollo 8 astronauts to "the people of earth" on Christmas Eve.[1]

Christmas is a time to thank God for his gifts to us and to give gifts to others. Therefore, at a typical Christmas Eve service, people read from the Bible about the birth of Jesus Christ—God's gift to Humanity that brings us joy and peace.

However, as the Apollo 8 astronauts orbited the moon on Christmas Eve, they read from the first chapter of Genesis. They reminded us that God created the heavens and the earth. They assured us that, after God created the earth, "God saw that it was good." They wished everyone a Merry Christmas. Then they closed their "Christmas Eve Service" by asking God to "bless all of you, all of you on the *good earth*."[2]

Through the eyes of the Apollo 8 astronauts, all humans saw the earth in a new way—as God's gift to Humanity . . . and we saw that it was good.

Through the eyes of the Apollo astronauts, we could see that the birthplace of Humanity was a "Garden of Eden"—a paradise that humans must cultivate with love.

The Bible warns us that "[w]here there is no vision, the people perish" (Proverbs 29:18, KJV).

Fortunately, in 1968, Apollo 8 gave us a new vision of the earth, Humanity, and God. It was a vision of the earth as a Garden of Eden—God's "Christmas present" to Humanity—a paradise that must not perish.

APOLLO 11

Apollo 8 gave us a new vision of the earth, Humanity and God. Apollo 11, however, gave us a new vision of the future.

When Apollo 11 landed on the moon, it left a plaque that said:

We came in peace for all mankind.[1]

As Neil Armstrong became the first person to set foot on the moon, a television camera beamed the moment back to hundreds of millions of people. Neil Armstrong told Humanity that he was making "one small step for a man, one giant leap for mankind."

At that moment, the earth became far more than a fragile blue and white oasis, hanging alone in the darkness. The earth became a lively, colorful cradle for a civilization that may span the heavens.

After Buzz Aldrin joined Neil Armstrong, the astronauts raised the Star Spangled Banner and planted it on the moon's surface. President Nixon called from the Oval Office in the White House to share his awe that: "For one priceless moment, in the whole history of man, all the people on this earth are truly one."

Armstrong replied that it was a great honor and privilege to be on the moon, "representing not only the United States but men of peace of all nations . . . men with a vision for the future."[2]
In the Apollo 11 vision of the future, Americans do not raise the Star Spangled Banner after killing people in battle—as the Marines did in World War II.

In the Apollo 11 vision of the future, Americans raise the Star Spangled Banner as they make giant leaps to reach New Frontiers. Americans raise the Star Spangled Banner as they set people free from Humanity's ancient foes: tyranny, poverty, disease and war itself. Americans raise the Star Spangled Banner as they come in peace for all mankind—for all Humanity.

Only Nixon Could Go to China

Unfortunately, the peace that we dreamed of when we landed on the moon disappeared in the nightmare of the Vietnam War. President Nixon strove mightily to end the war that he inherited from President Johnson, but to no avail.

Nixon became president in January, 1969, after winning a close election against Hubert Humphrey, who was Johnson's Vice President. Humphrey was a good and decent man, but he couldn't overcome his association with the inept and unpopular President Johnson.

There were two main reasons why Nixon won the election. First, people hoped that he would restore "law and order." This was an understandable desire after years of race riots, but it was also understandable that African-Americans saw the call for "law and order" as a euphemism for killing Martin Luther King's dream of racial equality and economic justice.

Second, people fondly hoped that Nixon had "a plan" for ending the Vietnam War. There was a historical basis for this hope. When President Eisenhower became president in 1953, with Nixon as his Vice President, the United States was trapped in a bloody stalemate in the Korean War. But within a year, the combination of President Eisenhower's threats to escalate the war (perhaps even using atomic weapons) and President Eisenhower's aggressive diplomacy brought a truce that has endured to this day (despite occasional violations). South Korea survived to become a stunning economic success story and an emerging democratic society.

Nixon tried to win a similar victory in South Vietnam by obtaining "peace with honor." His strategy involved training the South Vietnamese Army to replace United States troops, who were gradually withdrawing. To gain time for this strategy of "Vietnamization" to work, Nixon made greater use of United States military power, launching more powerful air attacks against North Vietnam and attacking Communist troops in their "sanctuaries." (This meant crossing the border into Cambodia. Cambodia was supposed to be a "neutral" country, but the Communists had been basing their army in Cambodia for years without fear of U.S. attack.)

In addition to such *military* moves in Vietnam, Nixon made *diplomatic* moves with China and the Soviet Union. He understood that the Vietnam War was a bitter fruit of the Cold War. Accordingly, the best way to bring a lasting peace in Vietnam was to ease tensions with North Vietnam's allies: China and the Soviet Union.

Therefore, Nixon took a bold risk that became *a giant leap forward* toward ending (and winning) the Cold War. Nixon went to China.

Nowadays, the fact that an American president would go to China and talk amiably with China's leaders doesn't seem like an earthshaking event. But during the height of the Cold War, Red China was seen as our most implacable foe. We had refused to accept the reality that the Communists had long ago won the Civil War against our allies, those Chinese who now only controlled the island of Formosa, today called Taiwan, off the coast of China.

Democrats were especially fearful of appearing to be "soft on China." This was because Republicans had criticized President Truman and his Secretary of State, George Marshall, for "losing China" to the Communists through their naiveté and ineptness after World War II.

Nixon launched his political career by warning about Communist spies and Communist plots. Therefore, "only Nixon could go to China." No Democrat could appear to trust Red China. But if that *Commie fighter* "Tricky Dick" Nixon thought that courting the Red Chinese was the smart thing to do, people conjectured, he *must* be right.

The Soviet Union was understandably alarmed that China (which shared a long, disputed border with the Soviet Union) was becoming friendly with the Soviet Union's other potential enemy, the United States. Nixon used this so-called "China card" to gain negotiating clout against the Soviet Union. The result was an easing of tensions with the Soviet Union that was called "detente" and that succeeded in slowing down the nuclear arms race.

When Nixon ran for re-election, he won a landslide victory over Senator George McGovern, who wanted the United States to end the Vietnam War immediately, even though South Vietnam would fall to the Communists. On the eve of the election, Nixon claimed that peace was "at hand" in Vietnam,[1] meaning that an agreement was about to be signed that would end the bloodshed and bring "peace with honor." Grateful Americans rewarded Nixon with another four years in office.

So what happened? Within a few years, Nixon resigned in disgrace and South Vietnam fell to the Communists. What went wrong?

Nixon went wrong.

As his nickname "Tricky Dick" signified, Nixon was never trusted by many Americans. And in the end, his deceitfulness brought him down in disgrace. First, it quickly became apparent after the 1972 presidential election that peace wasn't "at hand" in Vietnam.

Before long, Nixon was "carpet-bombing" North Vietnam in order to force them to sign a peace agreement. By late January, 1973, the North Vietnamese signed a cease-fire agreement, but Americans were left with the impression that Nixon had lied in order to win re-election.

Second, the economy had gone from bad to worse. The most damaging blow was the Arab Oil Embargo in the Fall and Winter of 1973. In retaliation for the support that the United States gave to Israel during the Yom Kippur War in October, 1973, Arab nations now refused to sell oil to the United States. Long lines formed at gas stations. Homes were cold that winter. Even outdoor Christmas lights were banned in a desperate effort to conserve fuel. People lost their jobs. It seemed natural that the President who'd caused the mess should lose his job, too.

Yet the final blow that crushed Nixon was called The Watergate Scandal. Nixon insisted that he had nothing to do with a break-in at the Democratic National Headquarters (held in the Watergate Hotel, Washington, D.C.) and a plot to plant wire-taps during the 1972 presidential campaign. At first, even most Nixon-haters believed his firm denials, if only because they thought that Nixon was far too smart to do anything so stupid. But after the election, the truth began to come out. Nixon had directed a "cover-up" of the break-in.

By August, 1974, when the truth became obvious, Republicans told Nixon to resign or the Congress would remove him from office. Nixon resigned. In hindsight, it is too easy to assume that America was destined to win the Cold War. People like to think that the Soviet Union was destined to collapse eventually because of the deep divisions among its people, its faltering economy, and the lack of trust that people had in their leaders.

But when Nixon resigned, it was *America* that looked as if it was collapsing. To the deep divisions that split America along racial lines were added the deep divisions about the Vietnam War. The economy was faltering. No one could trust a government that had lied again and again to the American people.

Why didn't America collapse? Much of the credit belongs to the wisdom of President Ford, to an emotional lift from the Bicentennial Celebration in 1976, and to the righteous leadership of President Jimmy Carter.

"WITH MALICE TOWARD NONE AND WITH CHARITY FOR ALL"

Not since President Truman took office during the onset of the Cold War had a new president faced as daunting a task as then Vice President Gerald Ford faced when he became The President of the United States after Richard Nixon resigned. Fortunately, Ford's wisdom carried him through the difficulty of leading a nation after a long, divisive war. He offered the same wise direction that Abraham Lincoln had to a divided America in seeking to heal its wounds after the Civil War: Act with malice toward none and with charity for all.

In the most controversial move of his presidency, Ford pardoned Richard Nixon for all of the crimes he had committed. At the time, his decision to pardon Nixon was immensely unpopular. But in hindsight, we can see the wisdom of ending the distraction of the Watergate Scandal so that the nation could concentrate on solving the problems that threatened America's survival: racial divisions, a faltering economy, and distrust of the government.

Ford also chose a wise path out of the Vietnam morass so that the nation could concentrate on solving the problems that threatened America's survival: racial divisions, a faltering economy, and distrust of the government. When the North Vietnamese took advantage of America's weakness to break the cease-fire agreement and launch a massive attack against South Vietnam, Ford didn't bomb the Communists or send U.S. troops back into Vietnam. He let events take their bitter course, ending in the quick collapse of South Vietnam to the triumphant Communists.

Like Truman, Ford was willing to make tough decisions. Ford was wise. And Ford was right.

THE BICENTENNIAL

During the Vietnam War, many people sneered at the very idea of patriotism. Many mocked the Star Spangled Banner. Some people even dared to burn the Star Spangled Banner in order to protest America's flawed policies and priorities.

Celebrating the Bicentennial on July fourth, 1976, changed all of that. Now that the Watergate Scandal and the Vietnam War were over, people were willing to celebrate the 200th birthday of America by remembering what they loved most about their country.

There was no single place where Americans celebrated the Bicentennial. Instead, television bound Americans together by displaying images from community to community, showing all the ways that people cherished their freedoms and loved America. For me, and for many Americans, the most memorable Bicentennial celebration was in New York City. By day, a huge fleet of majestic sailing ships graced New York's harbor. By night, a mammoth fireworks display lit up the harbor.

Television captured the awe-inspiring panorama. In the midst of the harbor—at the center of the celebration—stood the Statue of Liberty with her raised Torch of Liberty shining brightly. It was as if the Statue of Liberty was telling Americans not to despair. Despite our flaws, her Torch of Liberty was still shining in America and in our hearts.

With the light from her Torch of Liberty, after two hundred years as a nation, we saw America again. We heard America again. We understood the vision of America again.

SAINT JIMMY

America's trust in the Torch of Liberty was in part "born again" because her next president, Jimmy Carter, did his very best to live as a "born again" follower of Jesus Christ. After winning a close presidential election in 1976 against President Ford, Jimmy Carter went to work restoring Americans' trust in democracy. Carter was different. He wore sweaters instead of suits. He was always smiling. Most of all, he lived the way that people are supposed to live.

For years, Jimmy Carter taught the adult Sunday School class at the Baptist Church in his hometown of Plains, Georgia. He practiced what he preached. He was meek. He hungered and thirsted for righteousness. He was merciful. He was pure in heart (except that, as he once conceded to *Playboy* magazine, he sometimes "lusted in his heart" for women other than his wife). And he was a peacemaker.

There was never any doubt that Jimmy Carter was praying every day for God's guidance as he made so many difficult decisions. There was never any doubt that Jimmy Carter meant it when he said, "God bless America."

Despite being a white Southerner, Jimmy Carter befriended black people in their struggle for equal rights and justice long before it was politically popular to do so. He truly believed that all people are created equal by God and that God wants all people to enjoy life, liberty, and the pursuit of happiness—that is, Human Rights.

Slowly, under Carter the wounds caused by centuries of racism in America began to heal, even though the scars of racism would mar America for a long, long time. Carter turned the nurturing of Human Rights into the guiding principle of American foreign policy. He wanted America to help everyone in the world to enjoy life, liberty, and the pursuit of happiness. He wanted America's national security to depend on Humanity's love for the Torch of Liberty instead of on Humanity's fear of nuclear bombs.

Unfortunately, it seems that, as the old saying goes, "No good deed goes unpunished." And Jimmy Carter did so many good deeds that everything always seemed to be going wrong!

For example, the Middle East was the scene of both Jimmy Carter's greatest triumph and his greatest disaster.

His greatest triumph was the Camp David Peace Accord between Israel and Egypt. The picture of Jimmy Carter shaking hands with the smiling leaders of Egypt and Israel[1] as they ended decades of bloodshed gave people hope that Humanity's longing for peace was stronger than its lust for war.

However, not everyone in the Middle East liked America. And not everyone in the Middle East wanted peace with Israel.

Especially in Iran, there were bitter memories of a brutal regime that the United States imposed on Iran during the Cold War.

Moreover, many Iranians feared that the moral decadence of the United States (which they called "The Great Satan") was corrupting their Islamic culture. To humiliate America, the United States embassy in Iran was seized by terrorists who had the support of the Iranian government.

Despite everything that Jimmy Carter could do, Iran kept the hostages for 444 agonizing, humiliating days. Indeed, Iran hated Jimmy Carter so much that it refused to release the hostages until after he was no longer President.

Jimmy Carter's inability to end the Iranian Hostage Crisis successfully was a major reason why he lost the 1980 presidential election to Ronald Reagan. But it was not the only reason. Jimmy Carter was inexperienced. This led to many mistakes—real and perceived—in his decision-making at times.

Also, the U.S. economy was still in terrible shape. Inflation was running well over ten percent annually. There was scant economic growth. Standards of living were stagnant or falling. Jimmy Carter's medicines were high interest rates and the deregulation of some businesses—a program for curing America's economic ills about as popular as telling someone with high blood pressure to stop smoking, lose fifty pounds, and run five miles a day.

In the short run, Carter's economic policies inflicted great pain on America. In the long run, his policies laid the groundwork for Ronald Reagan's triumphs in the 1980s. Within a few years, high interest rates lowered inflation and fewer government regulations re-invigorated economic growth, especially when tied to Reagan's bold tax cuts. However, such long term benefits from Jimmy Carter's economic policies came far too late to help him win re-election.

Many people also feared that, in a dangerous world, Jesus's teachings in the Sermon on the Mount about meekness, hungering and thirsting for righteousness, showing mercy, being pure in heart, and being a peacemaker belonged in Sunday School instead of in the White House.

The Communists still couldn't be trusted—except to stir up trouble. The Soviet Union invaded Afghanistan and there was very little that a militarily and economically weak United States could do except rally world opinion against such blatant aggression.

To punish the Soviet Union, Jimmy Carter inadvertently hurt American athletes by boycotting the Olympics that were being held in Moscow. By cutting grain sales to the Soviet Union, he simultaneously hurt American farmers. In addition, despite his love for the idealism of the Sermon on the Mount, Jimmy Carter took some warlike steps that he knew were needed in a less than ideal world marred by sin: he helped the Afghan rebels in their guerrilla war against the Soviet Union and he began rebuilding America's military strength.

In the short run, Jimmy Carter's responses to the invasion of Afghanistan were immensely unpopular in America. However, in the long run, the war in Afghanistan became a Vietnam-style disaster for the Communists, contributing to the collapse of the Soviet Union.

Ultimately, America's peaceful victory in the Cold War proved that Jimmy Carter was right about the most important thing: the Torch of Liberty is the best weapon in America's arsenal.

MORNING IN AMERICA

Ronald Reagan was nicknamed "The Great Communicator" because of his unsurpassed skill in touching the hearts and minds of Americans. Another nickname should be "The Great Optimist" because it was ultimately Ronald Reagan's unflagging optimism that won the Cold War for America.

In his Inaugural Address, President Kennedy called upon America "to bear the burden of a long twilight struggle." By contrast, Ronald Reagan encouraged the nation with his conviction that it was "Morning in America." Reagan knew that America was still a young nation—full of energy and vitality. Therefore, said Reagan, America's future would be far greater than her past.

For decades, "foreign policy experts" had ingrained in Americans the pessimistic notion that, although we *might* be able to stop the spread of Communism, it was *impossible* to set a nation free after it had fallen into the steel grip of Communist tyranny. These "foreign policy experts" were certain that the Iron Curtain would always divide the free countries of Western Europe from the enslaved countries of Eastern Europe.

But Ronald Reagan was an optimist. He believed that the Torch of Liberty was shining in Humanity's heart throughout the world. He decided to launch an ideological and diplomatic offensive against Communism. He demanded that the Communists tear down the Berlin Wall, the hated symbol of the Cold War.

Soon after Reagan left office, his optimism bore fruit. Communism started collapsing with amazing speed. President George Bush (who had once been the head of the CIA and who had traveled the world for eight years as Reagan's Vice President) used his immense experience and skill in foreign policy to keep this revolution peaceful. As demonstrations mounted, Communist regimes vanished in Eastern Europe once the Soviet Union no longer propped them up.

For one brief, hopeful moment in June, 1989, it appeared that even Communist China might be ready to let her people be free. Brave protesters built a Statue of Liberty in Tiananmen Square (the Chinese equivalent of the Mall in Washington with its memorials to Washington and Lincoln). Unfortunately, the Communists found some unenlightened troops who followed their evil orders to kill the protesters and smash the Statue of Liberty.

Communists from the Soviet Union had used such barbarism to stamp out freedom in Hungary in 1956 and to crush liberty in Czechoslovakia in 1968. Barbarism prevailed again in China in 1989 as the world watched in shock and disbelief.

To this day, the Communist Chinese vainly hope that they can form a "union" with Taiwan and a "union" with the global economic community even though they do not give liberty to the Chinese people. Such cynicism did not work in America. And predictably, such cynicism will not work in China.

Liberty and union are one and inseparable, now and forever! Someday, the Statue of Liberty will stand tall again in Tiananmen Square.

The Torch of Liberty will triumph in China (despite Communist barbarism) just as the Torch of Liberty triumphed in Europe (despite Communist barbarism). In December, 1989, people celebrated the fall of Communist regimes throughout Eastern Europe by dancing atop the Berlin Wall. They then took sledgehammers and chisels to that hated symbol of tyranny.

Even after the fall of the Berlin Wall, the Communists hoped that they could hold on to power within the boundaries of the Soviet Union. But once again the Torch of Liberty was too strong for them. In December, 1991, the Soviet Union disbanded.

At long last, liberty *and* union had come to Europe, one and inseparable, now and forever.

On Christmas Day in 1991, Americans had a special reason to celebrate the joy and peace of Christmas. The flag of the Soviet Union came down in Moscow. The flag of a free Russia took its place. President Bush went on television to announce that—for the first time since the beginning of the Cold War decades earlier—America's nuclear weapons were no longer poised to launch a nuclear holocaust.

The optimism of Ronald Reagan and the diplomatic skill of George Bush won a peaceful victory in the Cold War, leading Humanity out of the Valley of the Shadow of a Nuclear Death.

"Morning in America" became Morning for all Humanity. Martin Luther King's dream was coming true. Brave, peaceful protesters had overcome evil with good—even when evil was supported by guns, tanks, and nuclear bombs.

As freedom rang throughout the lands that the Communists had tyrannized, people everywhere could say: "Free at last! Free at last! Thank God Almighty! We are free at last!"

PEACE FOR ALL HUMANITY

At the beginning of the Third Millennium, there were many celebrations. The greatest "celebration" of hope for the Future was the construction of the first International Space Station.

Actually, Russia and America have each had small space stations before this time. Now the former Cold War enemies are uniting to lead Humanity in the construction of a massive structure that will become the first true "settlement" in space.

If everything goes as hoped, there will never again be a time when all Humanity dwells on earth. From now on, Humanity will also dwell in the heavens! At this dawn of the Third Millennium after the birth of Jesus Christ, we have left the earth in order to live in the heavens—a giant leap forward for Humanity, as thrilling as when Abraham first left home for his New Frontier: the Promised Land.

It is fitting that the technologies of America, a nation of pioneers, now enable us to live on this New Frontier. But it is far more important that visions of America—the perfect America that was first seen in the hearts of Abraham, Moses, and Jesus—inspire us to live on this New Frontier.

Why? Because these bold visions of America inspire us to explore other New Frontiers where all people can be blessed. These visions of America inspire us to explore New Frontiers where people are set free from Humanity's ancient foes: tyranny, poverty, disease, and war itself.

These visions of America inspire us to explore New Frontiers where Good Samaritans bind the wounds of those in need, even if they have been taught to hate them because of their race, their nationality, or their religion. These visions of America inspire us to explore New Frontiers of Peace for all Humanity.

AFTERWORD

The first draft of *Visions of America* was completed on July fourth, 2001. As America peacefully celebrated the first Independence Day of the new millennium, little did we know that only a brief time remained before a terrorist attack on America on September 11, 2001 would shatter that peace.

Once again we've learned the hard lesson that despite our many past triumphs, we have only just begun to raise our Star Spangled Banner. To establish the work of our hands, we must raise our Star

Spangled Banner and lift our Torch of Liberty towards the heavens, despite the fact that our visions of America are not yet firmly planted in the earth.

Because even though the battle of the Cold War is won, the *war* against Sin is far from over:

- The War against all who are racists.
- The War against all who start wars.
- The War against all who persecute others.
- The War against all who love to hate.

America has come far. But America has much further to go.

We've only just begun to travel toward that Promised Land where all people will be blessed. We've only just begun to challenge the Pharaohs who refuse to let people be free. We've only just begun to sacrifice ourselves to help others.

Fortunately, our faith keeps us going no matter how bleak our lives may become. By hoping in the LORD, we find the faith to believe that the visions of Abraham, Moses and Jesus for America will be fulfilled, despite the fact that their visions of America are not yet firmly planted in the earth. By lighting the world with these visions of America, we show our faith that Humanity "shall be filled with the knowledge of the glory of the LORD, as the waters cover the sea." (Habakkuk 2:2–4, 14, KJV):

> And the LORD . . . said, Write the vision, and make it plain . . . [A]t the end [the vision] shall speak, and not lie; though it tarry, wait for it; because it will surely come, it will not tarry. [T]he just shall live by his faith. . . . For the earth shall be filled with the knowledge of the glory of the LORD, as the waters cover the sea. (Habakkuk 2:2–4, 14, KJV)

Visions of the Church
JOY AND PEACE

The Vision of the LORD:

The Experience of the Church:

Let the wicked forsake his way
    and the evil man his thoughts.
Let him turn to the LORD,
    and he will have mercy on him,
and to our God, for he will freely
    pardon.

"For my thoughts are not your
    thoughts,
neither are your ways my ways,"
    declares the LORD.
"As the heavens are higher than the
    earth,
so are my ways higher than your ways
and my thoughts than your thoughts.
As the rain and the snow come down
    from heaven,
and do not return to it without water-
    ing the earth
and making it bud and flourish,
so that it yields seed for the sower
    and bread for the eater,
so is my word that goes out from my
    mouth:
It will not return to me empty,
but will accomplish what I desire
and achieve the purpose for which I
    sent it.
You will go out in joy
    and be led forth in peace. . . .
            —Isaiah 55:7–13

"Houston, we've had a problem."
           —Apollo 13

CHAPTER 1

Getting Off the Launch Pad

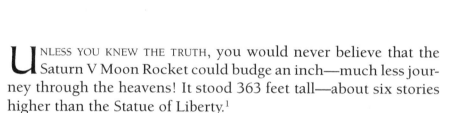

U NLESS YOU KNEW THE TRUTH, you would never believe that the Saturn V Moon Rocket could budge an inch—much less journey through the heavens! It stood 363 feet tall—about six stories higher than the Statue of Liberty.[1]

It weighed six million pounds.[2] Only a fool could think that something that big could move.

And unless you knew the truth, you would never believe that the Church could last a day—much less last two thousand years. Jesus was dead. His disciples hid in fear. One of them, Judas Iscariot, had betrayed him. One of them, Peter, had denied him.

Only a fool could think that people so weighed down by sin could hope to reach heaven.

Even so, despite such doubts, the Saturn V Moon Rocket launched towards the heavens on a pillar of fire amidst billows of smoke. And, despite such doubts, the Church launched out towards heaven on tongues of fire when the Holy Spirit filled the followers of Jesus Christ on the Day of Pentecost, fifty days after Jesus ascended to heaven.

The key was the hidden power that moved the Saturn V Moon Rocket and the hidden power that moved the Church. The Moon Rocket defeated the power of gravity by exploding chemicals inside the rocket. Jesus defeated the power of sin through his sacrificial death and his Resurrection. The shed blood of Jesus was the rocket fuel for his Church.

As foretold by an Old Testament prophecy:

> Surely he took up our infirmities and carried our sorrows. . . .
> [H]e was pierced for our transgressions, he was crushed for our
> iniquities; the punishment that brought us peace was upon him,
> and by his wounds we are healed, We all, like sheep, have gone
> astray, each of us has turned to his own way; and the LORD has
> laid on him the iniquity of us all. (Isaiah 53:4–6)

After the resurrection of Jesus Christ, he told his followers, "All authority in heaven and on earth has been given to me." He gave the church this mission: "[G]o and make disciples of all nations, baptizing them in the name of the Father and of the Son and of the Holy Spirit, and teaching them to obey everything I have commanded you" (Matthew 28: 18–20).

Jesus spoke these words, then ascended into Heaven, leaving a handful of followers to go and make disciples of all nations. This astounding development fulfilled another Old Testament prophecy in which God commanded people to repent—to change their way of life so that they would live in the way that God wants them to live:

> Let the wicked forsake his way and the evil man his thoughts.
> Let him turn to the LORD, and he will have mercy on him, and to
> our God, for he will freely pardon. (Isaiah 55:7)

God's willingness to forgive is totally different from our instinctive reaction when people hurt us. We want to strike back and hurt those who hurt us. But God is not like us. God loves everyone—even those who have gone far astray from God's ways. Indeed, ever since the first sin in the Garden of Eden, God seeks sinners to help them, even when they hide from him in fear (Genesis 3:8–10.)

Jesus showed this unquenchable love of God when he forgave those who crucified him. As he hung in agony on the Cross, he said, "Father, forgive them. . . ." (Luke 23:34).

By showing such a willingness to forgive, Jesus revealed the magnanimous way in which God loves to forgive us. The thoughts of Jesus were the thoughts of God—not the thoughts of sinful Humanity. And the ways of Jesus were the ways of God—not the ways of sinful Humanity.

This truth is stated beautifully in the words of the Old Testament prophet, Isaiah:

"For my thoughts are not your thoughts, neither are your ways my ways," declares the LORD. "As the heavens are higher than the earth, so are my ways higher than your ways and my thoughts than your thoughts." (Isaiah 55:8–9)

Next, Isaiah assures us that *God's* thoughts and *God's* ways will triumph. According to the prophecy, the word that goes out from the mouth of God is like the rain and the snow that come down from heaven. Just as the rain and the snow always make the earth bud and flourish, so God's Word will accomplish what God desires and achieve the purpose for which God sent it (Isaiah 55:10–11).

Jesus is the living Word of God (John 1:1–4,14). Therefore, teaching people to obey Jesus will accomplish what God desires and achieve the purpose of God. In the words of the Old Testament prophecy we are looking at here: "You will go out in joy and be led forth in peace" (Isaiah 55:12).

The first harvest of joy and peace came on the day that the Church was born—the day of Pentecost—a holiday that celebrates the beginning of the harvest (Exodus 23:16; Numbers 28:26).

In obedience to a command of Jesus Christ just before his Ascension into heaven, the disciples were waiting in Jerusalem until God the Father gave them "the gift of the Holy Spirit" (Acts 1:4–5). On the day of Pentecost, all of the followers of Jesus Christ were gathered in a house. Suddenly, as the Scripture tells it, there was a sound like a great wind blowing from heaven. Tongues of fire came to rest on each person. And "[a]ll of them were filled with the Holy Spirit" (Acts 2:1–4).

After this display of sound and fire worthy of the launch of a moon rocket, the disciples went forth into Jerusalem to proclaim the birth of the Church. In his sermon, Peter quoted an Old Testament prophecy that foretold what was happening:

> God says, I will pour out my Spirit on all people. . . . Even on my servants, both men and women, I will pour out my Spirit in those days. . . . I will show wonders in the heaven above and signs on the earth below, blood and fire and billows of smoke. . . . And everyone who calls on the name of the Lord will be saved. (Acts 2:16–21, quoting Joel 2:28–32)

The Church had cleared the launching pad. Its journey to bring joy and peace to all Humanity was now underway!

CHAPTER 2

Reaching Orbit

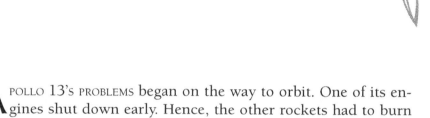

A POLLO 13'S PROBLEMS began on the way to orbit. One of its engines shut down early. Hence, the other rockets had to burn harder to make up the difference.

Fortunately, the astronauts reached orbit safely.

The Church's problems also began from its earliest moments. Lust for *money* led Christians astray. For example, James warned the early churches to stop showing favoritism to rich people (James 2:1–9). James condemned rich people for exploiting their workers (James 5:3–6). He knew that fights and quarrels were breaking out because people coveted things they could not get (James 4:1–2). People were asking God for things out of selfish motives so that they could spend what they got on their own pleasures (James 4:3). Meanwhile, they were not feeding and clothing poor people (James 2:15–16).

No wonder Paul taught that "the love of money is a root of all kinds of evil." Paul knew that "[s]ome people, eager for money, have wandered from the faith and pierced themselves with many griefs." Therefore, Paul warned the Church that "people who want to get rich fall into temptation and a trap and into many foolish and harmful desires that plunge men into ruin and destruction" (1 Timothy 6:9–10).

Lust for *sex* also led Christians astray. Paul condemned the church at Corinth for tolerating a member who was having sexual relations with his father's wife (1 Corinthians 5:1–5, 9–13). Paul also had to warn members of the church to stop engaging in sexual immorality, such as having sex with prostitutes (1 Corinthians 6:13–20).

Lust for *power* led Christians astray. For example, a Christian who had previously been a sorcerer tried to bribe Peter and John so that he could exploit the power of the Holy Spirit to do great signs and miracles (Acts 8:9–24). Paul and his mentor, Barnabus, quarreled so severely when they were planning a second missionary journey that they were unable to work together anymore (Acts 15:36–40). And Paul warned the church at Ephesus that members of their church would "arise and distort the truth in order to draw away disciples after them" (Acts 20:30).

Divisions between *cultures* caused divisions between *Christians*. For example, during the earliest days of the church in Jerusalem, members of the church who followed Greek cultural traditions complained that their widows were not receiving as much food as widows who followed Jewish cultural traditions (Acts 6:1). Years later, the clash of cultures was so great that Paul had to rebuke Peter publicly at the church in Antioch for refusing to eat with Christians who did not follow Jewish dietary rules (Galatians 2:11–16).

A council of church leaders that met at Jerusalem, including James, Peter, and Paul, reached a compromise between following Jewish cultural traditions and following Greek and Roman cultural traditions (Acts 15:22–29). Nevertheless, mistrust and suspicion continued between the Christians who followed Jewish cultural traditions and the Christians who followed Greek and Roman cultural traditions.[1]

Fortunately, there were also many Christians who obeyed what Jesus commanded because they were filled with the Holy Spirit. And there were courageous *martyrs*.

The first martyr we know of was Stephen. He was stoned to death outside of Jerusalem for denouncing the religious leaders who had killed Jesus. "While they were stoning him, Stephen prayed, 'Lord Jesus, receive my spirit.' Then he fell on his knees and cried out, 'Lord, do not hold this sin against them'" (Acts 7:51–60).

And there were tireless *missionaries*. Paul summed up his own experience as a missionary in this passage written to the church at Corinth:

> Five times I received . . . the forty lashes minus one. Three times I was beaten with rods, once I was stoned, three times I was shipwrecked. . . . I have labored and toiled and have often gone without sleep; I have known hunger and thirst and have often gone without food; I have been cold and naked. (2 Corinthians 11:24–27)

And there were generous *givers*. From the earliest days of the church at Jerusalem, "they gave to anyone as he had need" (Acts 2:45). A Christian in Joppa was beloved by everyone because she "was always doing good and helping the poor" (Acts 9:36). For example, she made "robes and other clothing" for widows (Acts 9:39). Churches sent help to other churches who were in need (Acts 11:27–30; Acts 24:17; 2 Corinthians 8:1–9:15).

There were compassionate *healers*. There was such confidence in the healing power of the early church in Jerusalem that "[c]rowds gathered . . . bringing their sick and those tormented by evil spirits, and all of them were healed" (Acts 5:16). Peter's success as a healer was so well known that "people brought the sick into the streets and laid them on beds and mats so that at least Peter's shadow might fall on some of them as he passed by" (Acts 5:15).

During his missionary journeys, Paul healed many people. At a city in Asia Minor, people were so impressed when Paul healed a man who had been crippled since birth that the crowd assumed that Paul was a god (Acts 14:8–18). To Paul's horror, the local priest of Zeus brought bulls and wreathes in order to offer pagan sacrifices to Paul! In another city, "God did extraordinary miracles through Paul, so that even handkerchiefs and aprons that had touched him were taken to the sick, and their illnesses were cured and the evil spirits left them" (Acts 19:11–12).

Inspired by the examples of such martyrs, missionaries, givers, and healers, the Church "reached orbit" within about 300 years by growing from a handful of believers in Jerusalem to become the dominant religion of the Roman Empire. Who accomplished this amazing, miraculous feat?

The names of a few people are known to us. But our knowledge of these first three centuries of the Church is mainly a tangle of history and legend that is hard to unravel two thousand years later.

In actuality, we should give the credit for this amazing, miraculous growth of the early Church to the Holy Spirit working through the "Unknown Christians." Just as nations honor those "Unknown Soldiers" who sacrificed their lives for their country, we should honor these Unknown Christians who lived in obscurity as faithful disciples of the Lord Jesus Christ.

CHAPTER 3

Preparing to Leave Earth Orbit

O NCE AN APOLLO SPACESHIP REACHED earth's orbit, it stayed in orbit for a few hours. This pause in the journey gave the astronauts time to prepare for the long ride to the moon. It was called "the parking orbit."

During this time, the astronauts checked their spaceship carefully to make sure that everything was fine. Only after this review of the spacecraft's condition would they ignite their rocket engine and head toward the moon.

In a similar fashion, the church paused in "earth orbit" for about a century after it became the official religion of the Roman Empire. After this period of relative peace and quiet, the Church faced renewed challenges when barbarians invaded and conquered the western half of the Roman Empire.

THE UNIVERSAL CHURCH COUNCILS

After three centuries of persecution, this was a golden chance to consolidate the Church and its teachings before the disasters that almost overwhelmed the Church when the barbarians invaded. During this time in "earth orbit," the basic doctrines of the Church

163

were summarized at Universal Church Councils that were called by Roman Emperors who were Christians.

The first such Universal Church Council was held in 325 at Nicaea. This gathering of about 230 bishops became known as the Council of Nicaea and was convened by the Emperor Constantine. He was the first Christian Roman Emperor. After winning a civil war, Constantine was eager to unify the Church in order to help unify the Roman Empire.

One key result of the Council of Nicaea was the adoption of the Creed of Nicaea, which provided the basis for what has become known as The Nicene Creed. This short statement of faith sets forth the key doctrines that all Christians must affirm.

The original Creed of Nicaea was written in Greek—the language used by influential Greek philosophers such as Plato, the language in which the New Testament was written, the language used by early Church theologians, and the language used for the deliberations at the Council of Nicaea.

It is difficult to translate the theological and philosophical subtleties of the Creed of Nicaea from Greek to English. Nevertheless, because the original Greek would be totally meaningless to people (such as myself) who do not read Greek, here is an English version of The Nicene Creed:

> I believe in one God the Father Almighty, Maker of heaven and earth, and of all things visible and invisible: And in one Lord Jesus Christ, the only–begotten Son of God, begotten of His Father before all worlds, God of God, Light of Light, very God of very God, begotten, not made, being of one substance with the Father, by whom all things were made; Who for us men and for our salvation came down from heaven, and was incarnate by the Holy Spirit of the Virgin Mary, and was made man, and crucified also for us under Pontius Pilate; He suffered and was buried, and the third day He rose again according to the Scriptures, and ascended into heaven, and sitteth on the right hand of the Father; And He shall come again with glory to judge both the quick and the dead; Whose kingdom shall have no end. And I believe in the Holy Spirit, the Lord and Giver of life, who

proceedeth from the Father and the Son, who with the Father and the Son together is worshiped and glorified; who spoke by the prophets. And I believe in one catholic and apostolic church; I acknowledge one baptism for the remission of sins, and I look for the resurrection of the dead, and the life of the world to come. Amen.[1]

The story of this key era in the development of the Church becomes even more complicated when it expands to cover the other Universal Church Councils that were convened by Roman Emperors from time to time over the next century.[2] The last such Universal Church Council was held at Chalcedon in 451. About 520 bishops attended.

These subsequent Universal Church Councils clarified the teachings of The Nicene Creed regarding central doctrines of the Christian faith. For example, the "Chalcedonian Definition" set forth a balanced compromise that clarified aspects of the incarnation of Jesus Christ. An English translation of the Chalcedonian Definition reads as follows:

Wherefore, following the holy Fathers, we all with one voice confess our Lord Jesus Christ one and the same Son, the same perfect in Godhead, the same perfect in manhood, truly God and truly man, the same consisting of a reasonable soul and a body, of one substance with the Father as touching the Godhead, the same of one substance with us as touching the manhood, like us in all things apart from sin; begotten of the Father before the ages as touching the Godhead, the same in the last days, for us and for our salvation, born from the Virgin Mary, the Theotokos [a Greek word meaning "God-bearer"], as touching the manhood, one and the same Christ, Son, Lord, Only-begotten, to be acknowledged in two natures, without confusion, without change, without division, without separation; the distinction of natures being in no way abolished because of the union but rather the characteristic property of each nature being preserved and concurring into one Person and one subsistence [hypostatsis] not as if Christ were parted or divided into two persons, but one and the same Son and Only-begotten God,

> Word, Lord, Jesus Christ; and our Lord Jesus Christ instructed us, and the Creed of the Fathers was handed down to us.[3]

These subsequent Universal Church Councils also refined decisions of the Council of Nicaea regarding issues such as the organizational structure of the Church, the canon of the Bible, the rituals for worship, and the giving of the sacraments. For example, one of the key issues was the relative importance and powers of the bishops of both Rome and Constantinople. Rome was the traditional capital of the Roman Empire. But Constantine, the first Christian Emperor, had founded Constantinople as a New Rome that would not be tainted by the original Rome's pagan past. On a more practical note, Constantine wanted this second capital of the Roman Empire in the eastern half of the Empire in order to strengthen his hold over these vast regions. (The eastern and western halves of the Roman Empire were gradually drifting apart, and the eastern and western halves of the Church reflected this gradual drift also.)

Therefore, on this touchy issue of the relative importance of the bishops of the two capital cities, the Council of Chalcedon adopted the following compromise language that gave Constantinople "equal privileges" with Rome, yet also said that Constantinople was "second after [the original Rome]":

> [T]he Fathers properly gave the primacy to the Throne of the elder Rome because that was the imperial city; and the 150 most religious bishops, being moved by the same intention, gave equal privileges to the most holy Throne of New Rome, judging rightly, that the city [Constantinople] which was honored with the sovereignty and senate which enjoyed equal privileges with the elder and Royal Rome should also be magnified like her in ecclesiastical matters, being the second after her.[4]

As you can begin to see, it would take an entire book to cover the Universal Church Councils adequately. Furthermore, one would need Ph.D. educations in philosophy, theology, ancient languages, Roman history, and Church history in order to fully understand the Universal Church Councils and their progressive decisions.

Only then could someone fully grasp the relevant teachings of the Scriptures, the mysteries of the theologians, the quarrels of the philosophers, and the passions of the politicians.

For our purposes, it will suffice to think of The Nicene Creed (and additional statements of faith that other Universal Church Councils adopted) as affirming the truth of Christmas and the truth of Easter . . . because these early creeds often focused primarily on the nature and meaning of the Incarnation, the death, and the Resurrection of Jesus Christ.

What is the truth of Christmas? What is the nature and meaning of the Incarnation of Jesus Christ? What is the truth of Easter? What is the nature and meaning of the death and Resurrection of Jesus Christ? It would take entire books to cover these truths that light the world—these visions of truth that light Humanity. Here are some highlights.

THE TRUTH OF CHRISTMAS

The truth of Christmas is that Jesus is fully God *and* fully human. And although this is a mystery that seems impossible, it is nevertheless true. How can it be? Because what is impossible with humans *is* possible with God (Luke 18:27).

The truth of Christmas is that Jesus is God Incarnate. One title that the Bible gives Jesus is "Immanuel," a name that means "God with us" (Matthew 1:22–23). Therefore, the God who spoke the heavens and the earth into being (Genesis 1) is also the Jesus who walked among us blessing children, welcoming sinners, weeping with those who weep, and washing the feet of those in need.[5]

The truth of Christmas is that God cares about each one of us. God is not merely far away tending the birth of new stars. God is near at hand, tending the birth of each baby.

God is not merely counting the millennia while Humanity gains technological prowess. God is counting the hairs on each person's head. God is not merely watching as the galaxy turns.[6] God is watching each sparrow that falls (Matthew 10:29–31).

The truth of Christmas is that each person is eternally, infinitely important. "[W]hoever welcomes a little child . . . welcomes [Jesus Christ]" (Matthew 18:5). There is a "kingdom prepared . . . since the creation of the world" for those who give a hungry person something to eat, those who give a thirsty person something to drink, who give shelter to a stranger, who give clothes to a needy person, who look after a sick person, or who visit a prisoner (Matthew 25:34–36). "[E]ternal life" awaits the person who performs such tiny acts of kindness. But "eternal fire" and "eternal punishment" await each person who neglects to perform such tiny acts of kindness as unto the Lord Jesus himself (Matthew 25:41–43, 46).

The truth of Christmas is that our lives have meaning. There is a true union between spiritual values and physical reality. Faith, hope, and love exist in history, not merely in myth.[7]

The truth of Christmas is that God is a person. That is why God could only be perfectly revealed to us by becoming flesh and dwelling among us as a person. And that is why we can only know God perfectly by having a personal relationship with God, our Friend.

We cannot be a friend to a human merely by thinking thoughts, learning facts, and following rules. We must laugh with our friend. We must weep with our friend. We must hope the best for our friend. We must hug our friend.

Similarly, we cannot be a friend to God merely by *thinking* thoughts, learning facts, and following rules. Being a friend to God requires the engagement of our whole personality—our laughter, our tears, our hopes, our hugs.

By living among us, Jesus revealed that God is such a person—such a friend to us. Jesus laughed.[8] Jesus wept (John 11:35). Jesus hoped (John 4:35), and Jesus hugged (Matthew 8:1–3; Mark 10:16).

The truth of Christmas—that Christ came in the flesh and God dwelt among us—brings peace on earth . . . and peace for all Humanity.

THE TRUTH OF EASTER

The truth of Easter is that Jesus rose from the dead. And although this historical fact seems impossible, it nevertheless is true. How can it be? Because what is impossible with humans is possible with God.

The truth of Easter is that our sins are forgiven. On the Cross, Jesus bore the punishment for our sins. Now, instead of suffering eternal death, we can enjoy eternal life. And because our sins are forgiven by God and forgotten by God, we can forget what is behind and press on toward what is ahead: "the prize of the high calling of God in Christ Jesus" (Philippians 3:13–14, KJV).

The truth of Easter is that we need no longer fear death. We should weep at the tombs of those we love just as Jesus wept at the tomb of Lazarus (John 11:35). However, we should not grieve like those who have no hope (1 Thessalonians 4:13). For we believe that we shall meet again those who have fallen asleep in Jesus. We will laugh with them again. We will hug them again (1 Thessalonians 4:13–18).

The truth of Easter is that *there is always hope* (Job 14:7). No matter how much it looks as if we have failed. No matter how much it looks as if evil has triumphed. There is still hope. Therefore, we must still keep the faith (2 Timothy 4:7). We must still keep loving (Matthew 24:12–13). Because, in God's good time and in God's good way, God will bring good from evil (Genesis 50:19–20; Exodus 7:3–5), healing from suffering (Job 42:1–6; Isaiah 53:4–5, 10–12), and life from death (Ezekiel 37:1–14; 1 Corinthians 15:12–26). *How?*

Although this is impossible for humans, it is possible for God. For "in all things God works for the good of those who love him" (Romans 8:28). Nothing "shall separate us from the love of Christ." Not "trouble or hardship or persecution or famine or nakedness or danger or sword" (Romans 8:35). "[I]n all these things we are more than conquerors through him who loved us. For . . . neither death nor life, neither angels nor demons, neither the present nor the future, nor any powers, neither height nor depth, nor anything else in all creation, will be able to separate us from the love of God that is in Christ Jesus our Lord" (Romans 8:37–39).

The truth of Easter gives joy to the world—joy for all Humanity!

St. Augustine

The most famous Christian from this Roman era of Church history is St. Augustine.[1] He was born in North Africa in 354. His father worshipped the Roman gods and his mother worshipped God the Father, Son, and Holy Spirit. St. Augustine was a pagan for much of his early life. He became a disciple of Jesus Christ at about the age of 30.

The story of the spiritual journey that took St. Augustine from paganism to Christianity is told in his famous book, *Confessions*. In the pages of his personal confession to God, Augustine describes the lusts that enslaved him until he found freedom through faith in Jesus Christ. He also describes the intellectual doubts that he had about the truth of Christianity until he believed in Jesus Christ.

As he looked back on the long and winding road that had led to his conversion to Christianity, St. Augustine saw how the fervent, patient prayers of his mother for his salvation were answered by the providence and grace of God. His years of searching for the truth ended in a moment of sudden revelation and conversion. As he described that moment in his *Confessions*, he speaks of experiencing an emotional and spiritual crisis as he realized his utter inability to control his lusts:

> I probed the hidden depths of my soul and wrung its pitiful secrets from it, and when I mustered them all before the eyes of my heart, a great storm broke within me, bringing with it a great deluge of tears. . . . For I felt that I was still the captive of my sins.

> I was . . . weeping all the while with the most bitter sorrow in my heart, when all at once I heard the sing-song voice of a child in a nearby house. Whether it was the voice of a boy or a girl I

cannot say, but again and again it repeated the refrain "Take it and read it, take it and read." At this I looked up, thinking hard whether there was any kind of game in which children used to chant words like these, but I could not remember ever hearing them before. I stemmed my flood of tears and stood up, telling myself that this could only be a divine command to open my book of Scripture and read the first passage on which my eyes should fall . . .

So I hurried . . . and in silence I read the first passage on which my eyes fell: Not in reveling and drunkenness, not in lust and wantonness, not in quarrels and rivalries. Rather, arm yourselves with the Lord Jesus Christ; spend no more thought on nature and nature's appetites. I had no wish to read more and no need to do so. For in an instant, as I came to the end of the sentence, it was as though the light of confidence flooded into my heart and all the darkness of doubt was dispelled.[2]

It would be more than a thousand years until the hymn was written that best describes St. Augustine's experience of God's grace. But since with God a thousand years passes as quickly as if it were a single day (Psalm 90:4; 2 Peter 3:8), we should not be surprised that St. Augustine in Roman times experienced the truth about God's amazing grace that Christians of today sing about in the hymn "Amazing Grace":

> Amazing grace! How sweet the sound—
> that saved a wretch like me!
> I once was lost, but now am found,
> was blind, but now I see.
>
> 'Twas grace that taught my heart to fear,
> and grace my fears relieved;
> how precious did that grace appear
> the hour I first believed.[3]

In the finest Roman tradition, St. Augustine was well educated in the ways of rhetoric and in the arts of government. Accordingly, he soon became the bishop of Hippo, a city in North Africa, where he ministered for the remaining forty years of his life.

St. Augustine was such a skillful debater and gifted writer that he found himself constantly explaining why Christianity was the truth. He was also brilliant at explaining the interrelationship between Christian beliefs and the main philosophical beliefs of his culture, especially the ideas of ancient Greek philosophers such as Plato.

St. Augustine's ideas are preserved in many books, the most impressive of which is *The City of God*. In this monumental work that took fourteen years to complete, St. Augustine first refuted traditional Roman religious beliefs. He then showed how all of history could be seen as a struggle between two cities: an earthly city full of lusts and a heavenly city full of love.

It is fascinating to speculate how much St. Augustine's long struggle against lust in his personal life gave him the insights needed for his monumental depiction of the struggle between good and evil in the heavens and upon the earth. St. Augustine's seemingly futile struggle against sin in his own life ultimately culminated in the triumph of good. And in *The City of God*, Augustine shared his faith that the seemingly futile struggle against sin in the heavens and upon the earth will ultimately culminate in the triumph of good—in the heavens and on earth.

Writing in an era when Christians were savoring their triumph over paganism and when the Roman Empire was enjoying one last "Indian Summer" before the winter of the barbarian conquests, St. Augustine gave us a vision of the future of the Church that is glorious and triumphant.

As he reached the end of writing *The City of God*, St. Augustine realized that the ultimate destiny of the City of God—which in our era is the Church—is to be "delivered from all ill, filled with all good, enjoying . . . the delights of eternal joys."[4] When we at last know that "peace of God which . . . passeth all understanding"[5] we shall enjoy "eternal repose not only of the spirit, but also of the body. There we shall rest and see, see and love, love and praise. This is what shall be in the end without end. For what other end do we propose to ourselves than to attain to the kingdom of which there is no end."[6]

Just as the first two verses of "Amazing Grace" perfectly describe that moment when St. Augustine first experienced God's joy and peace in his own life, the final verse of "Amazing Grace" perfectly describes those endless ages that St. Augustine envisioned when the City of God—*the Church*—will experience God's eternal joy and peace:

> When we've been there ten thousand years,
> Bright shining as the sun,
> We've no less days to sing God's praise
> Than when we'd first begun.[7]

CHAPTER 4

"Houston, We've Had A Problem"

WHEN APOLLO 13 WAS 200,000 miles from earth, the astronauts heard "a loud, dull bang." The whole spaceship shuddered. The master alarm rang. Red warning lights started going off and on. The astronauts urgently radioed mission control, "Houston, we've had a problem."

Back at mission control, the experts struggled to figure out what had happened.

At first, mission control hoped that nothing was actually wrong with the spaceship. Communications had been disrupted so perhaps the alarming data being received from the spaceship was garbled. Or perhaps there was only a minor problem with a few instruments that were sending false warning signals when, in fact, everything was fine. Such false alarms had happened before on spaceflights, after all.

But then, the astronauts radioed back that they could see a gas of some sort venting from the Service Module. As problems mounted with the spaceship, all doubt was soon gone: disaster had struck Apollo 13.

One TV commentator went on the air. Preparing viewers for the worst, he warned that the astronauts had only about a 10 per cent chance of making it home alive.

At first, some people speculated that a meteor might have struck Apollo 13, causing the malfunction that led to disaster. But later, when all the evidence was in, it was determined that the fault lay inside the spaceship itself. A problem with a fuel cell had caused the explosion that ripped through the Service Module of the spaceship, knocking out the rocket engine and the life support systems.[1]

DISASTER STRIKES THE CHURCH

Little did St. Augustine know that his writings and his life reflected not only the strengths of a triumphant Church, but also the weaknesses of a troubled Church.

For example, St. Augustine wrote in Latin. He knew little Greek. Therefore, his knowledge of the early Greek theologians of the Church was limited to the translations of their writings that were available to him. Similarly, his knowledge of Greek philosophers was based solely on Latin translations that could not capture perfectly the original ideas of the authors. A chasm was opening between the eastern half of the Church (where Constantinople led churches that used Greek) and the western half of the Church (where Rome led churches that used Latin).

Furthermore, the Roman Empire was beginning its own catastrophic decline, which led to the victory of barbarism in the western half of the Empire. Rome was sacked by the Goths in 410. This calamity (which would have been unthinkable during the long centuries when Rome "ruled the world") led St. Augustine to begin writing *The City of God.* He wanted to refute claims by pagans that the rise of Christianity caused the sack of Rome because Rome's gods were unhappy.

Another sign of decay surfaced in 430: an army of invading Vandals besieged Hippo as St. Augustine lay dying. As the centuries passed, some Christians tried to ignore signs that the Church was not living up to the standards of conduct that Jesus set, much as Mission Control hoped at first that nothing was actually wrong with Apollo 13.

Then, when Christians could no longer ignore some of the terrible things that some of their fellow Christians were doing—such as starting wars, oppressing and exploiting people—some Christians tried to excuse the Church by blaming outside forces for their shameful deeds:

- It was the fault of barbarians.
- It was the fault of heretics.
- It was the fault of poverty.
- It was the fault of ignorance.

Just as Mission Control wanted to blame an outside factor, such as a meteor, for the problems with Apollo 13, Christians wanted to blame anyone and anything other than themselves for the problems within the Church.

But the truth is that the underlying problem with the Church was the problem of sin. The Church itself was flawed by sin because the people who made up the Church were flawed by sin.

WHO IS THE GREATEST?

What were these intractable problems with the Church? What were these *flaws* caused by sin? As with any historical event—and especially any historical event that spans centuries—there are many ways to answer such a question.

For example, the verse of the Bible that St. Augustine read when he became a Christian exhorted us to arm ourselves with the Lord Jesus Christ so that we could stop committing a wide variety of sins: reveling and drunkenness, lust and wantonness, quarrels and rivalries. As we've already seen, from the earliest days of the Church Christians have been led astray by a lust for money, a lust for sex, and a lust for power. Furthermore, from the earliest days of the Church, divisions among cultures have caused divisions among Christians.

While all of this makes a fascinating study in itself, I'd like to focus on the problem of "quarrels and rivalries" among Christians.

To be sure, many of these "quarrels and rivalries" have been the bitter fruit of the lust for money, the lust for sex, the lust for power, and divisions between cultures. However, the most fundamental problem lies with a quarrel and rivalry that began among the disciples even while Jesus still walked among them: Who is "the greatest?"

> [A]n argument started among the disciples as to which of them would be the greatest. Jesus, knowing their thoughts, took a little child and had him stand beside him. Then he said to them, 'Whoever welcomes this little child in my name welcomes me; and whoever welcomes me welcomes the one who sent me. For he who is least among you all, he is the greatest.'" (Luke 9:46–48).

Or, as Jesus put it another time when the disciples were indignant because two of their number, James and John, wanted to be greater than any of the other disciples:

> "You know that those who are regarded as rulers [of nations] lord it over [others], and their high officials exercise authority over [others]. Not so with you. Instead, whoever wants to become great among you must be your servant, and whoever wants to be first must be slave of all. For even the Son of Man did not come to be served, but to serve, and to give his life as a ransom for many." (Mark 10:41–45)

Jesus also had to warn his disciples against using *force* to destroy those who disagreed with them. One day Jesus wanted to visit a Samaritan village. But the Samaritans rejected Jesus because the Samaritans hated Jews and Jesus was a Jew on his way to Jerusalem. "When the disciples James and John saw this, they asked, 'Lord, do you want us to call fire down from heaven to destroy them?' But Jesus turned and rebuked them . . ." (Luke 9:51–55).

Nevertheless, Christians throughout the centuries have persisted in arguing among themselves about who is, was, or will be

the greatest. Christians have even resorted to force in order to coerce and destroy those who've disagreed with them.[1]

One example of such a sin was the sacking of Constantinople
in 1204. We have already seen how the Council of Chalcedon established an uneasy compromise between Rome and
Constantinople regarding which city's church leadership would
have the greatest power and influence. But the religious leaders in
the original capital of the Roman empire and in the *new* capital of
the Roman empire were *not* willing to follow Jesus' advice to become "the least" so that they would become "the greatest."

This sinful rivalry between Rome and Constantinople reached
its tragic climax when Christian Crusaders sacked Constantinople
in 1204.[2] The Christians of the West (who obeyed the Pope in
Rome) sent an army of Crusaders to help recapture the Holy Land.
But instead, the army ended up attacking the Christians of the
East (who obeyed the patriarch in Constantinople). The Christians of the west were motivated by the sin of pride to prove that
they were the greatest. The Christians of the West were also motivated by the sin of greed to plunder the wealth of Constantinople.

As a result of this fighting among Christians, the remnant of
the Roman Empire in the East (a Christian empire called the Byz-
antine Empire) was fatally weakened. In 1453, Constantinople fell
to an Islamic army.[3] As Islam advanced through the Balkans towards Central Europe, it began to look as if Christianity were
doomed.

Christianity did not appear to be doomed merely because Islam's
armies were mightier than its own. The spiritual fire seemed to
have gone out of Christianity. Christians had fallen prey to the lust
for money, the lust for sex, and the lust for power. They were no
longer fit to follow Jesus Christ's command to "go and make disciples . . . teaching them to *obey everything* I have commanded
you" (Matthew 28:19–20, emphasis added).

It appeared impossible for the Church to survive. But what is
impossible with humans is possible with God. Within a few decades, Christopher Columbus had discovered America, bringing
the wealth of the New World to strengthen Europe and setting

Western Civilization on the road to becoming the first culture to dominate the entire globe.

Even more importantly, the Church experienced a Great Awakening. Thus, as Western Civilization spread across the globe at this key moment in the history of Humanity, Christians were able to fulfill the commission given to them by Jesus Christ: "[G]o and make disciples of all nations, baptizing them in the name of the Father and of the Son and of the Holy Spirit, and teaching them to obey everything I have commanded you" (Matthew 28:19–20).

CHAPTER 5

Relying Upon the Lunar Module

T HE SERVICE MODULE WAS DYING. Without the electricity from the Service Module, the Command Module could not function. The astronauts would die.

Without the rocket engine from the Service Module, the Command Module was on a course that would never return to earth. The astronauts would die.

Only one small hope remained. Flee to the Lunar Module. Use its electricity and oxygen to stay alive during the trip to earth. Use the rocket on the Lunar Module to get the astronauts on a course towards earth. And hope that enough electricity remained in the batteries in the Command Module so that the astronauts could restart the Command Module at the critical moment just before they reentered earth's atmosphere.

Only the strength of the Command Module could survive the fiery plunge through earth's atmosphere that would come at the end of the voyage. The paper-thin walls of the Lunar Module could not survive the heat and the stress from such a fiery trial.

No wonder that the TV anchorman gave the astronauts only a 10 percent chance of reaching home alive.

But desperate times demand desperate measures. So the astronauts turned off the Command Module and crammed themselves into the Lunar Module . . . while back home, people despaired and prayed.

St. Francis of Assisi

In 1204, Christians should have despaired and prayed. In the struggle to prove who was "The Greatest," the army of the Western Christians fought the army of the Eastern Christians at Constantinople. The Western Christians "won," sacking the city, plundering its ancient wealth and smashing its incomparable beauty.

Fortunately, the prayers of Christians for a future full of faith, hope, and love began to be answered around 1205 when a young man in Italy decided to become the least in the Kingdom of Heaven. He renounced all the wealth and lusts of the world. Living in absolute poverty, begging for his food, he traveled from place to place, preaching the Good News about Jesus Christ.[1]

This "least of the least" is known to us as St. Francis of Assisi.

St. Francis of Assisi, and countless others like him through the centuries, have been the "Lunar Module" of the Church that kept the Church alive while the rich and powerful failed her. By becoming "The Least" in the Kingdom of Heaven, they actually became "The Greatest."

With the Service Module and the Command Module of the spacecraft crippled, the Lunar Module seemed hopelessly unequal to the task that lay ahead. Its walls were aluminum foil. It was only big enough for two people. Now it would have to keep three people alive. It was designed to land on the moon. Now it would have to journey between the moon and the earth.

Similarly, it would seem impossible that lowly St. Francis of Assisi, who lived in extreme poverty, could be far greater than entire armies of soldiers dying in battle. But what is impossible for humans is possible with God. Indeed, "God chose the foolish things of the world to shame the wise; God chose the weak things of the world to shame the strong" (1 Corinthians 1:27).

This is why the Old Testament prophet wrote, "'For my thoughts are not your thoughts, neither are your ways my ways,' declares the Lord. 'As the heavens are higher than the earth, so are my ways higher than your ways and my thoughts than your thoughts. (Isaiah 55:8–9) '"

And so God chose the weakness of St. Francis of Assisi instead of the strength of armies to spread his Kingdom on this earth—his Church. *Why?* Because God's "strength is made perfect in weakness" (2 Corinthians 12:9, KJV). That is also why God chose the weakest of the weak—a young mother, Mary, and her tiny baby, Jesus, to bring joy and peace to Humanity.

Armies of Christians fighting with swords at Constantinople almost destroyed the Church. Meanwhile, St. Francis of Assisi's "tiny" acts of kindness infused the Church with new life. That is why there is a "kingdom prepared . . . since the creation of the world" for those who give a hungry person something to eat, who give a thirsty person something to drink, who give shelter to a stranger, who give clothes to a needy person, who look after a sick person, who visit a prisoner (Matthew 25:34–36) or who in some other way serve and honor God.

St. Francis of Assisi found the perfect way to dramatize this truth of Christmas. He invented the Nativity Scene.[2]

The Nativity is simple. A homeless family. A humble stable. A loving mother. A faithful husband. A tiny baby. Lowly shepherds. Lordly kings. Bleating sheep. Singing angels.

Yet the Nativity is profound. God is with us, even when we are poor and find ourselves in "humble stables." The lowliest family is blessed. Poor people worship God. Rich people worship God. Nature worships God. Heaven worships God. This vision is brilliant in its simplicity.

And while the victories won with swords at Constantinople led to disaster for all Christians, the words that God spoke through St. Francis of Assisi still bless us today. Because God has promised:

As the rain and the snow come down from heaven, and do not return to it without watering the earth and making it bud and flourish, so that it yields seed for the sower and bread for the eater, so is my word that goes out from my mouth: It will not return to me empty, but will accomplish what I desire and achieve the purpose for which I sent it. You will go out in joy and be led forth in peace . . . (Isaiah 55:10–12)

The life of St. Francis of Assisi shows us the truth of Easter. Although it appeared impossible for the Church to survive the flaws and misguided direction of Christians, God resurrected the Church at its darkest hour using the most unlikely of people—a poverty-stricken beggar preaching the Good News about Jesus Christ.

The good news that St. Francis of Assisi preached is the truth of Christmas and the truth of Easter. We can find God's blessings even in the most unlikely, or in the most desperate, circumstances because of the joy that comes from following Jesus Christ, God's Christmas gift to Humanity. We can live in harmony with God, Humanity and nature—all creatures of our God and King—because of the peace that comes from following Jesus Christ, God's Christmas gift to Humanity.

We can spend our lives going out in joy and being led forth in peace by experiencing the truth of these words that God spoke through St. Francis of Assisi almost a thousand years ago:

> All creatures of our God and King,
> Lift up your voice and with us sing
> Alleluia, Alleluia!
> Thou burning sun with golden beam,
> Thou silver moon with softer gleam.
> O praise him, O praise him,
> Alleluia, Alleluia, Alleluia!
>
> And all ye men of tender heart,
> Forgiving others, take your part,
> O sing ye, Alleluia!
> Ye who long pain and sorrow bear,
> Praise God and on Him cast your care,
> O praise him, O praise him,
> Alleluia, Alleluia, Alleluia!

Let all things their Creator bless,
And worship Him in humbleness,
O praise him, Alleluia!
Praise, praise the Father, praise the Son,
And praise the Spirit, Three in One,
O praise Him, O praise Him,
Alleluia, Alleluia, Alleluia![3]

CHAPTER 6

Flying the Spaceship

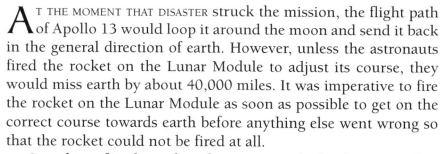

A T THE MOMENT THAT DISASTER struck the mission, the flight path of Apollo 13 would loop it around the moon and send it back in the general direction of earth. However, unless the astronauts fired the rocket on the Lunar Module to adjust its course, they would miss earth by about 40,000 miles. It was imperative to fire the rocket on the Lunar Module as soon as possible to get on the correct course towards earth before anything else went wrong so that the rocket could not be fired at all.

In order to fire the rocket, the astronauts had to be certain that the spaceship was oriented correctly in space. Otherwise, they'd fire the rocket in the wrong direction and make things even worse than they already were.

As the Command Module was shutting down, the astronauts raced to copy the navigational data from the computer in the Command Module into the computer in the Lunar Module. Normally, the astronauts could double-check the computer by taking sightings of the stars, just as navigators on ships had navigated for centuries. But at the moment it was impossible to see any navigational stars. A cloud of gas and debris surrounded the spaceship, blocking any view of the stars.

With help from Mission Control in Houston, the astronauts double checked their arithmetic as they entered the data (adjustments to the data had to be made to account for the different orientation of the Lunar Module compared to the Command Module).

With this task accomplished, the astronauts fired the engine on the Lunar Module. It worked perfectly.

Still, they would be much more confident that they were on the right course if they could see the stars to check their location. At last, someone thought of using the one star that they still *could* see—our own sun. Eureka! Checking their course against the sun confirmed their position.

The astronauts successfully looped around the moon and began coming closer to earth. Nevertheless, the situation remained grim. On their current course, it would take too long to reach home. It was by no means certain that the supplies on the tiny Lunar Module, designed to keep only two men alive on the moon, could keep three men alive long enough to get home. Therefore, the astronauts fired the rocket on the Lunar Module a second time, speeding their return to earth so that they would reach it safely in time.

Then Mission Control radioed more grim news to the astronauts. For some unknown reason, the spaceship was drifting off course. It was essential to be precisely on course because, if they entered the atmosphere at too steep an angle, the heat and stress would crush the Command Module. On the other hand, if they entered the atmosphere at too shallow an angle, the Command Module would skip off the atmosphere back into space like a stone skipping off the water. So, whether the Command Module entered the atmosphere too steeply or too shallow, the end result was the same: the crew died.

Instead, the astronauts must fire the rocket on the Lunar Module a *third* time in order to get back precisely on course. But there was a big problem. To conserve electricity, the astronauts had shut off their computer as soon as they finished firing their rocket the second time. There was no way to use the computer to navigate. The astronauts would have to find another way.

This time they navigated by first orienting themselves towards the sun and then towards the earth. They centered the earth in the crosshairs of a special gunsight that was normally used for rendezvous maneuvers. Mission Control assured them that as long as they kept their gunsight fixed on the earth, they'd be firing their rocket in the right direction to reach the planet safely.

To be successful, all three astronauts had to work together flawlessly. One turned on the rocket. One kept the spaceship correctly oriented. One counted the seconds so that the rocket burned for the right amount of time. And, amazingly . . .

It worked! Apollo 13 was back on course, heading towards its plunge through earth's atmosphere. Working together, the crew would make it home—and live.

God

The voyage of Apollo 13 took only a few days.

The voyage of the Church from the Fall of Rome (the 400s) to the Rise of America (1776) took more than 1000 years. In one key aspect, however, the voyage of Apollo 13 and the voyage of the Church were the same: God did the impossible.

During the voyage of Apollo 13, our utter dependence upon God is best illustrated by the role of gravity in getting the spaceship back to earth. It was the moon's gravity that bent the spaceship's path back toward the course that it needed to take to reach earth, which represented life. And it was the earth's gravity that accelerated the spaceship as it neared the planet so that the trip was completed quickly enough to save the crew before supplies ran out. Compared to the immense role of gravity in shaping the spaceship's destiny, the effect of the rockets was puny, at best.

Similarly, it was God's amazing grace that bent the Church's path back toward the course that it needed to take to reach heaven— the destination representing eternal life. And it is God's amazing grace that is accelerating the voyage of the Church so that the days of its voyage will be shortened enough for Humanity to survive despite the ravages of sin (Matthew 24:22).

Compared to the immense role of God's amazing grace in shaping our personal destinies and the destiny of the Church, our efforts are puny, at best. Full credit belongs to the power of God the Father, Who determines the destiny of each of us and of the entire Church.

Indeed, as we discussed when describing the launch of the immense Saturn V rocket, even the "rockets" of our own effort are actually the result of the amazing grace of God. The "fuel" for our rockets is the Blood of God the Son, Jesus Christ—the Blood that Jesus voluntarily shed to save us from our sins through his amazing grace. "For God so loved the world that he gave his one and only Son, that whoever believes in him shall not perish, but have eternal life" (John 3:16).

And while the Father determines our destiny and the Son provides us fuel for the voyage, the Holy Spirit comforts and guides us along our journey. To please God, we must follow Jesus Christ in the way that brings us "righteousness, peace, and joy in the Holy Spirit" (Romans 14:17–18). This is our true "home."

THE UNKNOWN CHRISTIANS

Across this immense span of generations, only a handful of Christians are remembered. Most of the people whose righteousness, joy, and peace lighted the centuries from the Fall of Rome until the Rise of America are Unknown Christians.

The cathedrals that are scattered throughout Europe are our most fitting monuments to these Unknown Christians. Two of my favorites are found in the heart of Paris: Sainte-Chapelle and Notre Dame.

Actually, Sainte-Chapelle is so tiny that it may not even qualify as a true cathedral. Nevertheless, it is a stunning monument to the yearning of people to touch the beauty of eternity. I do not believe that there is any sight on earth more beautiful than the stained glass windows of Sainte-Chapelle in the sunlight. The infinite value of such fragile beauty speaks of the infinite value of each person's fragile life and of each person's fragile quest for eternal life.

Truly, when we stand amidst the color and light of Sainte-Chapelle's windows, we feel the truth of Christmas—the truth that we mere mortals can experience the infinite beauty of God through the windows of our souls.

And where Sainte-Chapelle is awesome in its *fragile* beauty, Notre Dame is awesome in its *majestic* beauty. The strength of stone walls, pillars, and arches speaks of the infinite strength of the majestic Church that God is building.[1]

When we stand amidst the soaring buttresses of Notre Dame's gothic arches and contemplate the beauty of its ancient Rose Window, we feel the truth of Easter–the truth that we mere mortals *can* experience eternal life through the strength of God that empowers us to gaze forever on the majestic beauty of his holiness. Here, our soul finds "home."

St. Thomas Aquinas

Fortunately, we do know the names of *some* of the Christians who steered the Church on its journey across the millennia from the Fall of Rome to the Rise of America. And few names from this era shine more brightly than the name of St. Thomas Aquinas.

Just as the astronauts desperately copied the data from their computer in the Command Module onto their computer in the Lunar Module, medieval Christians copied ancient books and studied them. Around the time of Aquinas, a major body of ancient knowledge was recovered by Christians in Western Europe: the ancient Greek writings of Aristotle.

Aristotle's writings became available again from translations made by Arab scholars. It was no small task to understand this body of philosophy and to reconcile it with Christian theology. Aquinas was perhaps the greatest scholar to undertake the challenge.

Curiously, Aquinas was born at almost the same time as St. Francis of Assisi died. Much of his life was spent in Paris, where the leading scholars of his time frequently gathered. In the Paris that Aquinas knew, Sainte-Chapelle, with its stunning stained glass windows, was slowly being built. Meanwhile, a short distance away, the cathedral of Notre Dame was also under construction. It was only about halfway finished. It took more than two centuries to complete Notre Dame using plans that an unknown architect, an Unknown Christian, bequeathed to succeeding generations.

Aquinas did not bequeath to future generations the plans for a Church built with stone. Instead, Aquinas bequeathed the vision of a Church built with joy and peace. According to *this* vision of the Church, we have joy and peace because Jesus Christ died for our sins and reconciled us to God. As Aquinas put it:

> ... to unite men to God belongs to Christ, through whom men are reconciled to God (2 Corinthians 5:19): "God was in Christ reconciling the world to himself." And so only Christ is the perfect mediator of God and men, in that through his death he reconciled the human race to God ...

> [Because] Christ by suffering out of love and obedience gave to God more than was required to compensate for the offense of the whole human race. First, by reason of the tremendous charity from which he suffered; second by reason of the dignity of his life, which he gave up in atonement, for this was the life of one who was both God and man; third, on account of the extent of the passion and the greatness of the sorrow suffered. . . . And so Christ's passion was not merely a sufficient but a superabundant atonement for the sins of the human race: according to "He is the propitiation for our sins; and not for ours only, but also for those of the whole world" (1 John 2: 2).[1]

Words such as *mediator, atonement,* and *propitiation* have a rather formal, legalistic, intimidating tone. A more "user-friendly" way to understand the joy and peace of Christians is to realize that the Holy Spirit enables us to become friends of God. As Aquinas put it:

> In friendship we quite rightly delight in the friend's presence, are happy with what he says and does, and find our security in

every worry so that we normally rush to friends for consolation in time of sorrow. Because the Holy Spirit makes us friends of God, whom he brings to abide in us and us in him, it is therefore through the Holy Spirit that we experience joy in God as well as security amidst earthly troubles and temptations. And so the Psalmist says: "Restore unto me the joy of thy salvation and strengthen me with thy lordly Spirit" (Psalm 50:14); and (Romans 14:17): "The Kingdom of God is not meat and drink; but justice, and peace, and joy in the Holy Spirit"; and (Acts 9: 31): "The Church had peace and was edified, walking in the fear of the Lord, and was filled with the consolation of the Holy Spirit."[2]

MARTIN LUTHER

The longer Apollo 13 traveled without checking the computer's data against the actual location of the stars, the more likely it became that the spaceship was losing its way. Similarly, the further the Church traveled from the time of Jesus without checking its teachings against the authority of the Bible, the more likely it became that the Church was losing its way.

The cloud of debris that surrounded Apollo 13 continued to make it impossible to see the stars. Fortunately, Mission Control found a way to check Apollo 13's *actual* orientation compared to its computer-derived orientation. They told the astronauts to check their orientation with relation to the sun, and everyone was elated to find that the spaceship's actual orientation indeed matched its computer-derived orientation. Applause broke out in Mission Control!

Similarly, a cloud of spiritual debris sometimes surrounds the Church, making it impossible to see how God wants us to live. This is debris from the lust for sex, the lust for money, the lust for power, the divisions between cultures, and the quarrels and rivalries that come from wanting to be "The Greatest."

Nevertheless, Martin Luther found a way to check the Church's actual orientation compared with its tradition-derived orientation. More than two hundred years after Aquinas lived, Martin Luther told us to check our beliefs and our actions in relation to the "perfect navigational star" in the Bible. Only then, said the Catholic priest-turned-reformer, can we know whether we are on the right or the wrong course spiritually.

But there the similarity with Apollo 13 ended. Martin Luther did not find that the course that the Church was on was correctly oriented. No applause broke out after his study of the Bible. For example, the Church had become corrupt through its lust for money—the sale of "indulgences," which promised to forgive sins in return for money! (This may sound somewhat "far out" now, but are some of the common practices of today really much different?)

Comparing the reality of the way Christians were living with the way that the Bible said we *should* live showed Luther just how far the Church had gone astray—just how far the Church had drifted off course—like a herd of sheep slowly straying from their shepherd. And so Martin Luther sounded the alarm, nailing his famous "95 Theses" to the church door at Wittenburg, Germany, in 1517.

Fortunately, Luther not only used the Bible to diagnose the disease. Martin Luther also used the Bible to show us the cure for all of our sins: the amazing grace of God. And Martin Luther learned from the Bible how this cure worked: by faith in Jesus Christ.

Apollo 13 corrected its course and hastened its journey home by igniting the engine on the Lunar Module a second time. And because the spaceship was oriented correctly, the astronauts succeeded in returning home.

In the Church's journey across the millennia, Martin Luther ignited the rocket engine of faith. And because the Bible enables the Church to orient itself correctly, the Church will succeed in its mission. The amazing grace of God through faith in Jesus Christ will keep us on course and bring us home in time.

Here is how Luther understood the kind of faith that ignites our lives and enables the Church to live the way that we *should* live on our journey toward eternal life:

To Luther, faith was not primarily intellectual assent. . . . It was, rather, the grateful, whole-hearted response of one's entire being to the love of God in Christ: it was full confidence in God.

Indeed, Luther believed that justification was by faith alone . . . and that . . . Augustine had said it before him. Experience and study had led [Luther] to the conviction that man could never earn God's favor by good works of any kind. . . . He did not discount good works, but to his mind they do not earn justification but are the fruits of faith, the response in gratitude and love to the love of God in Christ.[1]

By his own account, here is how Luther experienced the faith in Christ that leads to righteousness, joy, and peace:

I began to comprehend the "righteousness of God" through which the righteous are saved by God's grace, namely, through faith; that the "righteousness of God" which is revealed through the Gospel was to be understood in a passive sense in which God through mercy justifies man by faith, as it is written, "The just shall live by faith." Now I felt exactly as though I had been born again, and I believed that I had entered Paradise through widely opened doors.[2]

JOHN WESLEY

After the second perfect firing of the Lunar Module's engine, Mission Control thought they had Apollo 13 back on course. Then, to their horror, they saw that the spaceship was straying off course! Immediately, they knew that, as impossible as it seemed, the engine must be fired again.

But the computer was turned off. How could the astronauts, first of all, even orient the spaceship? This time the astronauts used both the sun and the Earth. Then they kept their gunsight looking straight at the earth all the time that they fired the engine.

In one respect, John Wesley was far more fortunate than the astronauts of Apollo 13—the Church's "computer" still worked.

As John Wesley oriented the Church and ignited its engine more than two hundred years after Martin Luther lived and died, he could still use the same "computer" as Aquinas used. By reading the books that had been so carefully copied, John Wesley absorbed the wisdom of many saints and the learning of many scholars, stretching back to the time of Jesus and the apostles. For example, John Wesley loved to study the writings of St. Augustine.

In addition, Wesley shared Martin Luther's passion for using the Bible as the authoritative benchmark for determining the way that we should live on our journey toward eternal life. Like Luther, John Wesley knew that faith in Jesus Christ was the only way to get people's lives and the life of the Church back on course.

Nevertheless, John Wesley was troubled for years by his overwhelming fear of death. He worked and worked at being a good person and at converting others to Christianity, yet he did not experience the assurance that he himself was destined for heaven instead of for hell.

How could John Wesley find such assurance? How could John Wesley find such peace and joy? Only through the Holy Spirit.

After years of searching for assurance, peace, and joy, John Wesley found them when he felt the Holy Spirit take control of his life. This moment of spiritual enlightenment came, for him, during a meeting of believers at Aldersgate, England. He recorded what happened in his daily journal.

> The speaker was reading Luther's preface to the Epistle to Romans—the book of the Bible that Martin Luther was studying when he realized that "the righteousness of God" can only be achieved through God's amazing grace by faith in Jesus Christ.
>
> John Wesley explained in his journal that, as the speaker described, "the change which God works in the heart through faith in Christ, I felt my heart strangely warmed. I felt I did trust in Christ, Christ alone, for salvation; and an assurance was given me that He had taken away my sins, even mine, and saved me from the law of sin and death."[1]

John Wesley had found the way to live that leads to eternal life. And he spent the rest of his life igniting the faith of the Church and pointing the Church in the way that it should go.

CHARLES WESLEY

John Wesley was an organizational genius. The success of Methodism is traced to his tireless efforts and skill in organizing his followers.

But the contribution of his brother, Charles Wesley, was also essential to the Church. Indeed, as the centuries dim the organizational successes of *John* Wesley, it is the hymns of *Charles Wesley* that are the most enduring legacy of the revival that both John and Charles Wesley led.

For example, Charles Wesley's hymn "And Can It Be" helps all people to experience the joy and peace that come when our hearts are "strangely warmed by the Holy Spirit":

> And can it be that I should gain
> An int'rest in the Savior's Blood?
> Died He for me, who caused His pain?
> For me, who Him to death pursued?
> Amazing love! How can it be
> That Thou, my God shouldst die for me?
>
> He left His Father's throne above,
> So free, so infinite His grace!
> Emptied Himself of all but love,
> And bled for Adam's helpless race!
> 'Tis mercy all, immense and free,
> For, O my God, it found out me.
>
> Long my imprisoned spirit lay
> Fast bound in sin and nature's night.
> Thine eye diffused a quick'ning ray:
> I woke—the dungeon flamed with light!
> My chains fell off; my heart was free,

I rose, went forth, and followed Thee.

No condemnation now I dread:
Jesus, and all in Him is mine!
Alive in Him, my living Head,
And clothed in righteousness divine,
Bold I approach th'eternal throne,
And claim the crown, through Christ my own.

Charles Wesley's hymn "Hark The Herald Angels Sing" still helps all people to experience the truth of Christmas:

Hark! The herald angels sing,
"Glory to the newborn King;
Peace on earth, and mercy mild,
God and sinners reconciled!"
Joyful, all ye nations, rise,
Join the triumph of the skies;
With th'angelic host proclaim,
"Christ is born in Bethlehem!"
　　Hark, the herald angels sing,
　　"Glory to the newborn King."

And his hymn "Christ the Lord Is Risen Today" helps all people to experience the truth of Easter:

Christ the Lord is ris'n today, Alleluia!
Sons of men and angels say: Alleluia!
Raise your joys and triumphs high, Alleluia!
Sing, ye heav'ns, and earth reply: Alleluia!

Love's redeeming work is done, Alleluia!
Fought the fight, the battle won, Alleluia!
Death in vain forbids Him rise, Alleluia!
Christ has opened paradise, Alleluia!

Soar we now where Christ has led, Alleluia!
Foll'wing our exalted Head, Alleluia!

Made like Him, like Him we rise, Alleluia!
Ours the Cross, the grave, the skies, Alleluia!

THE CHURCH

The astronauts of Apollo 13 learned that the key to reaching home was to keep their gunsight firmly fixed on the earth—the beginning and the end of their journey. And as Christians, we must keep our "gunsight" firmly fixed on Jesus Christ: "Looking unto Jesus, the author and finisher of our faith" (Hebrews 12:2, KJV).

The astronauts of Apollo 13 also learned that the only way to reach home was to work together. To fire their engine successfully this third time, each astronaut performed a task that only he could perform. One astronaut controlled the engine. One astronaut described the location of the earth so that the engine could fire in the right direction. And the third astronaut counted the seconds out loud so that the engine would burn for exactly the right amount of time.

Similarly, the only way for the Church to stay on course is for all Christians to work together. Keeping our eyes fixed on Jesus requires all of the Church—all of the Body of Christ—to strive together in unity. Each Christian must perform a task that only *that* Christian can perform.

Some must be like Aquinas, harvesting the wisdom of saints and the learning of scholars across the millennia. Some Christians will be like Martin Luther, applying the Bible as the authoritative benchmark of right and wrong. Others must be like John Wesley, sharing the assurance that the Holy Spirit gives.

Some Christians must be like Charles Wesley, using their artistic skills—whether as songwriters, painters, sculptors, or architects—to help us experience joy and peace. And all Christians must be like the "Unknown Christians," willing to labor in total obscurity to build the Church for the glory of God. Building "Sainte-Chapelles" and "Notre Dames." Experiencing the truth of Christmas and the truth of Easter. Admiring the fragile beauty of each life and the majestic beauty of the Church.

CHAPTER 7

Resurrecting the Command Module

TIME WAS RUNNING OUT! And a daunting task faced the Apollo 13 astronauts.

They must restart the Command Module. Usually, the complicated task of powering up the Command Module took a full day, a team of technicians, and unlimited amounts of electricity.[1] Now three astronauts must do it using unfamiliar procedures, within only a few hours, and with no electricity to spare. There was barely enough power in the batteries of the Command Module to get it running again, keep it running through the fires of reentry, and open its parachutes for a safe landing in the ocean.

Making the task even more difficult was the poor physical condition of the astronauts. They were exhausted and cold. Amidst the cold and the stress, no one could sleep soundly. One astronaut even suffered from an infection and a high fever.

The condition of the Command Module was far from perfect. With almost all of the electricity turned off, the spaceship was very cold. After sitting cold and unused for days, the Command Module was soaking wet with dew. A single flaw in the wiring would mean that the water on the wires could short out the whole electrical system, dooming the craft's cramped inhabitants. The final straw was that the spaceship was again drifting off course!

At the time, the reason for this frustrating, terrifying problem of straying from the way home was unknown. After the flight, engineers figured out what had happened. It seems a small amount of water vapor routinely vented from the Lunar Module's cooling system. During the short descent to the lunar surface and while the vehicle rested on the moon, this small amount of venting wasn't a problem. But during the long coast back toward earth, even this small amount of venting was pushing the spaceship off course.[2]

Against all odds, the astronauts did the impossible. They resurrected the "dead" Command Module by turning its systems back on and getting it back on course—just in time for it to undergo the fiery trial of passing through the earth's atmosphere. They were on the way home again.

The Loss of Faith, Hope, and Love

As the Church approached the close of the Second Millennium, it appeared that time was running out to prepare for the fiery trials that lay ahead. While Jesus walked among us, he assured us that, although there would be wars and rumors of wars, we should not be alarmed. The end is still to come. Such problems are merely the beginning of birth pains for the new heaven and the new earth that will be born (Matthew 24:6–8). Nevertheless, the Twentieth Century witnessed horrors so daunting that Humanity seemed doomed.

The butchery of two world wars showed the depths to which humans would descend in seeking power. The cruelty of the Holocaust revealed the depths to which humans would descend in persecuting people of other races and religions. And now this violent "civilization" possessed enough nuclear weapons to make of the earth a vision of hell forever.

It seemed the Church was once again straying off course due to people's unbridled lust for sex, lust for money, and lust for power—in addition to divisions between cultures and to quarrels and rivalries that come from wanting to be "The Greatest."

Small wonder that many people lost their faith in, their hope in, and their love for God.

Fortunately, countless Unknown Christians kept faith, hope, and love alive. Indeed, God's power was made perfect in many of them *because* they experienced weakness (2 Corinthians 12:9). For example, the Church in the Soviet Union emerged triumphant from seventy years of persecution by the Communists. And the Church in China is growing today despite continued persecution by the Communist regime in power there.

We may never know the names of those *unknown* martyrs, missionaries, givers, and healers who have filled the underground Church with the power of faith, hope, and love despite bitter persecution by Communists. However, we *do* know the names of three *famous* Christians who filled the Church with the power of faith, hope, and love in such dark times for Humanity: Billy Graham, Martin Luther King, Jr., and Mother Teresa.

BILLY GRAHAM: FAITH

Billy Graham preached for decades about the faith in Jesus Christ that can put people and the Church back on course toward eternal life. Two of his favorite passages from the Bible are the story of the Prodigal Son (Luke 15:11–32) and the story of the Rich Young Ruler (Matthew 19:16–22; Luke 18:18–25).

The Prodigal Son is an example of a person who has strayed so far off course that he or she will hit the earth's atmosphere at too steep an angle—burning up from lusts. As you may recall, the Prodigal Son left his father's home in order to indulge his lusts. But when he ran out of money, his "friends" deserted him and he found himself close to starvation. At last, he decided to go home. His father forgave him, welcoming him warmly, showing us that even the person whose lusts have "ruined his or her life" *can* find forgiveness from God and get their life back on course for eternity.

The Rich Young Ruler had the opposite problem. He was the kind of person who has strayed off course so that he or she will hit the earth's atmosphere at too shallow an angle—bouncing off into the icy cold darkness of space. As you may recall, the Rich Young Ruler was very careful to keep the Ten Commandments. But he still did not choose to follow Jesus . . . because he loved something *more* than Jesus—his money. Therefore, when Jesus commanded him to sell all of his riches, give the money to the poor, and come, follow Him, he went away in sorrow.

Going to church regularly and following the rules of good behavior aren't enough to keep us on course toward eternal life. We must follow Jesus with our whole heart, loving nothing—and no one—more than Him. We must have faith in Jesus Christ, enough to obey and follow Him.

The preaching of Billy Graham encouraged millions of people to find the faith in Jesus Christ that enables them to flee their lusts, to put God first in their lives, and to follow Jesus daily.

Martin Luther King, Jr.: Hope

Martin Luther King, Jr. faced a seemingly hopeless struggle. For centuries, African-Americans had been persecuted and exploited. Nevertheless, he was determined to help them.

Martin Luther King, Jr. faced *another* hopeless struggle. For millennia, poor people had been despised and exploited. Nevertheless, he was determined to help them.

Martin Luther King, Jr. faced a *third* hopeless struggle. For millennia, people had fought wars. Nevertheless, he was determined to help end wars and find peace.

There were many times in these hopeless struggles when Martin Luther King, Jr. knew discouragement and defeat. Nevertheless, the night before he was killed, this Baptist preacher spoke words of hope and encouragement to all Humanity. The hope that his dreams of joy and peace bring is worth remembering again:

> Well, I don't know what will happen now. We've got some difficult days ahead. But it really doesn't matter with me now, because I've been to the mountaintop. And I don't mind. Like anybody, I would like to live a long life. Longevity has its place. But I'm not concerned about that now. I just want to do God's will. And He's allowed me to go up to the mountain, and I've

looked over, and I've seen the Promised Land. I may not get there with you. But I want you to know tonight, that we as a people will get to the Promised Land. And so I'm happy tonight. I'm not worried about anything. I'm not fearing any man. Mine eyes have seen the glory of the coming of the Lord.[1]

MOTHER TERESA: LOVE

Mother Teresa enabled countless poor, suffering, dying people to see the glory of the coming of the Lord. Her ministry in Calcutta to (as she referred to them) "The Least of Humanity" made her among "The Greatest" of the Church.

Hear her wisdom about the power of love:

What we need is to love without getting tired. How does a lamp burn? Through the continuous input of small drops of oil. What are these drops of oil in our lamps? They are the small things of daily life: faithfulness, small words of kindness, a thought for others, our way of being silent, of looking, of speaking, and of acting. . . .

These words of Jesus, "Even as I have loved you that you also love one another," should be not only a light to us, but they should also be a flame consuming the selfishness that prevents the growth of holiness. Jesus "loved us to the end," to the very limit of love: the Cross. This love must come from within, from our union with Christ. Loving must be as normal to us as living and breathing, day after day until our death.[1]

Mother Teresa's wisdom unites the truth of Christmas with the truth of Easter: the power of love comes from the perfect union between each person *giving* love to others in the smallest things of daily life (the "Least Things") and each person *receiving* the gift of Christ's limitless love on the Cross (the "Greatest Thing").

To have power in the Church, we need "faith, hope and love. But the greatest of these is love" (1 Corinthians 13:13).[2]

CHAPTER 8

Reaching Home

JUST BEFORE HITTING THE ATMOSPHERE at 25,000 miles per hour, the Apollo astronauts jettisoned the Service Module, exposing the Command Module's heat shield. The heat shield needed to protect the astronauts from temperatures that would soon soar to 5,000 degrees centigrade![1]

As the Service Module tumbled away, the astronauts were stunned by the damage they saw. It was far worse than they'd imagined. They thought there might be a small hole in the Service Module. Instead, an entire side of the Service Module was blown away, exposing its shambled innards.

The realization of just how badly the Service Module had been damaged heightened a nagging worry within the crew members: had the explosion cracked the heat shield? Because, if there was a big crack in the heat shield, the astronauts knew they *would* burn up during the fiery trial that lay ahead.

Hoping for the best, the travelers strapped themselves onto their couches. In a gesture of respect, the mission commander gave up his seat to the astronaut who would have to pilot the Command Module during this crisis. Now, all Humanity waited, hoping and praying that we'd see television pictures of Apollo 13 reaching home safe and sound.

Miraculously, our prayers were answered. All Humanity cheered as television pictures showed the capsule floating triumphantly down from the sky on its billowing parachutes. Our joy was complete when we saw the astronauts emerge safe and sound from the Command Module.

Similarly, as Christians look back on two thousand years of Church history, we are stunned by how badly our sins have damaged the Service Module. We've damaged the Church far more than we'd imagined. And so the nagging worry is heightened: Have we damaged the Church so badly that we will burn up during the fiery trial that lies ahead? Are the divisions in the Church so great that these cracks in our *heat shield* doom us? Has the struggle to be *The Greatest* doomed us all?

Fortunately, everything is possible with God. Indeed, he has already told us how to heal these rifts and divisions: acknowledge them. We must confess our sins because "[i]f we confess our sins, he is faithful and just and will forgive us our sins and purify us from all unrighteousness" (1 John 1:9). As we confess, God will purify us from our lust for sex, our lust for money, our lust for power, our divisions between cultures, and the quarrels and rivalries that come from wanting to be "The Greatest."

Then we must put into practice the wisdom that Jesus tried to teach his disciples when he walked among us. "Whoever wants to be the leader must be the servant." To be "The Greatest," we must become "The Least" among those who serve.

Just as the Commander of Apollo 13 gave up his rightful seat so that another person could fill that position in the best interests of the mission, we must be willing to give up our rightful position in the Church so that other persons can use their talents in the best interests of the Church.

After all, Jesus Christ was the first person to show us that becoming *The Least* is the best—indeed, the only—way to become *The Greatest*. Although Jesus was "in very nature God," he "did not consider equality with God something to be grasped, but made himself nothing, taking the very nature of a servant . . ." Furthermore, "he humbled himself and became obedient to death—even death on a cross! Therefore, God exalted him to the highest place and gave him the name that is above every name . . ." (Philippians 2:5–9).

Our "heat shield" can protect us because "we are more than conquerors through him who loved us." Therefore, nothing "will be able to separate us from the love of God that is in Christ Jesus our Lord" (Romans 8:37–39).

Furthermore, our "heat shield" can protect us because it is made from the same "armor of God" that Paul told Christians to rely on two thousand years ago:

> Stand firm . . . with the belt of truth buckled around your waist, with the breastplate of righteousness in place, and with your feet fitted with the readiness that comes from the gospel of peace. In addition to all this, take up the shield of faith, with which you can extinguish all the flaming arrows of the evil one. Take the helmet of salvation and the sword of the Spirit, which is the word of God. (Ephesians 6:11, 14–17).

By using the sword of the Spirit, we can be certain that we will find joy and peace. The sword of the Spirit is the Word of God, and God has promised that his Word will accomplish the purpose for which he sent it, enabling us to "go out in joy and be led forth in peace" (Isaiah 55:13).

Therefore, just as the world's last visions of Apollo 13 were the best ones—the Command Module floating majestically down from the sky on its billowing parachutes and the astronauts coming forth safely from the Command Module—our last visions of the Church will be the best ones ever yet beheld.

In these visions of a new heaven and a new earth in the Book of Revelation, we see "the Holy City, the new Jerusalem, coming down out of heaven from God, prepared as a bride beautifully dressed for her husband." We "will be his people, and God himself will be with [us] and will be [our] God, [wiping] every tear from [our] eyes" (Revelation 21:2–4).

In these prophetic visions of the perfect joy and peace to come, we will "dwell in the house of the LORD forever" (Psalm 23:6). It is the house of that LORD who is a faithful husband and a loving father—a Friend who is always with us, and Who wipes away each tear from our eyes.

CHAPTER 9

Celebrating

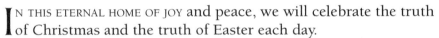

IN THIS ETERNAL HOME OF JOY and peace, we will celebrate the truth of Christmas and the truth of Easter each day.

To celebrate when the astronauts reached home, some people in Mission Control lit cigars. However, to celebrate when the Church reaches home, instead of lighting a cigar, I'd like to light a candle just as we do once each year in our church on Christmas Eve.

At the culmination of our Christmas Eve Service, it is dark except for a few candles at the altar. Each person waits in their pew with an unlit candle. Then the light symbolizing Jesus Christ is passed from candle to candle until the whole church is lit by the warm glow of candlelight. Together we sing "Silent Night" and "Joy to The World," lifting our candles high in celebration.

That moment of celebration lasts for only a few moments. However, when we've been celebrating in the City of God for ten thousand years, with our candles shining "bright as the sun," we'll have "no less days to sing God's praise than when we'd first begun." And we'll be glad that we have an eternity to celebrate. *Why?*

We'll always love to sing about that silent night, that holy night, when Jesus Christ, the Truth of Christmas, gave us peace on earth–Peace for all Humanity!

And we'll always love to sing about that happy morning, that amazing morning, when Jesus Christ, the Truth of Easter, gave joy to the world—Joy for all Humanity!

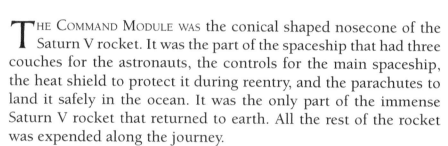

APPENDICES:
A Description of the Apollo Moon Missions

THE COMMAND MODULE WAS the conical shaped nosecone of the Saturn V rocket. It was the part of the spaceship that had three couches for the astronauts, the controls for the main spaceship, the heat shield to protect it during reentry, and the parachutes to land it safely in the ocean. It was the only part of the immense Saturn V rocket that returned to earth. All the rest of the rocket was expended along the journey.

The Service Module was attached to the back of the Command Module next to the heat shield. It contained supplies for the journey, including oxygen to breathe, fuel cells to generate electricity, and rocket fuel. It also contained the rocket engine for the spaceship. The nozzle of the rocket engine extended out the back of the Service Module. Astronauts could not enter the Service Module. The Service Module itself was jettisoned just before reentering earth's atmosphere. It burned up during reentry.

The Lunar Module was nicknamed the "spider" because that was what it looked like. It had a rocket engine for landing on the moon. The lower stage of the Lunar Module remained on the moon, serving as a launch pad for the upper portion of the Lunar Module that contained the two astronauts who actually landed on the moon's surface, got out, and walked around. The third astronaut remained in orbit around the moon in the Command Module.

At liftoff, the Lunar Module was behind the Service Module, perched atop the uppermost stage of the Saturn V (that stage shut down upon reaching earth orbit, then restarted in order to send the spacecraft to the moon). A short time after leaving earth orbit, the Command Module (with the Service Module attached) separated from the uppermost stage of the Saturn V and turned around to connect the top of the Command Module to the top of the Lunar Module. After docking headfirst with the Lunar Module, the Command Module pulled the Lunar Module away from the uppermost stage of the Saturn V rocket.

The uppermost stage of the Saturn V rocket was then sent on a different pathway toward the moon so that it wouldn't collide with the manned spaceship. This now consisted of the Command Module in the middle of the Service Module and the Lunar Module. A cylindrical corridor connected the Command Module to the Lunar Module. The astronauts floated in zero gravity "up and down" this corridor in order to go between the Command Module and the Lunar Module.

The "United States" Compared to "America"

In my books, I use the terms "United States" and "America" differently.

The term "America" is the term that I use for the ideal community that is composed of Christians *and* non-Christians. As I discuss in *Visions of America, Visions of the Church*, America is that ideal community that was first discovered in the hearts of Abraham, Moses and Jesus–a community of good neighbors. Therefore, anyone in the world who seeks to implement American ideals can be an American regardless of their religion, nationality or citizenship.

In contrast, I use the term "United States" to refer to the actual, historical political entity that exists today as the "United States of America." Unfortunately, the actual, historical United States of America is marred by Sin and falls short of being the ideal America envisioned by Abraham, Moses and Jesus because all humans (except Jesus–the Holy One of Humanity) "have sinned and fall short of the glory of God" (Romans 3:23).

Similarly, *Visions of America, Visions of the Church* describes visions of the ideal community called the Church that is composed *exclusively* of Christians–a community of best friends. It also describes ways that the actual, historical Church has been marred by Sin and falls short of being that ideal community

215

because all Christians (except Jesus–the Holy One of Humanity) "have sinned and fall short of the glory of God" (Romans 3:23).

Endnotes

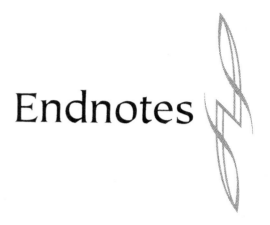

Book One: Visions of America
I. The Great Awakening

Visions of America
1. The phrase "the Good Earth" comes from Apollo 8, the first manned spaceship to orbit the moon. See my discussion of the impact of Apollo 8 on the environmental movement later in this book.

The Great Awakening
1. Oscar Theodore Barck, Jr. and Hugh Talmage Lefler, Colonial America, 2d ed. (New York: Macmillan, 1968), 402.
2. Ola Elizabeth Winslow, ed., Jonathan Edwards: Basic Writings (New York: New American Library, Signet Classic, 1966), 150, 160, 161, 164 (emphasis in original).
3. See President Kennedy's Inaugural Address: "Let every nation know, whether it wishes us well or ill, that we shall pay any price, bear any burden, meet any hardship, support any friend, oppose any foe, to assure the survival and the success of liberty."

Lexington and Concord
1. My discussion of the Puritans and the English Civil War is based upon my general knowledge of the subject, supported by information in Barck and Lefler, Colonial America, 83–86, and Winston S. Churchill, The New World,

Vol. 2 of A History of the English-Speaking Peoples (New York: Dodd, Mead & Company, 1956), 147–334 .

The Declaration of Independence

1. My discussion of the American Revolution is based upon my general knowledge of the subject, supported by information in Barck and Lefler, Colonial America and Winston S. Churchill, The Age of Revolution, Vol. 3 of History of the English-Speaking Peoples, 139–213.
2. My discussion of Jefferson drafting the Declaration of Independence is based upon my general knowledge of the subject, supported by information in William Sterne Randall, Thomas Jefferson: A Life (New York: Henry Holt and Company, 1993; New York: Harper Collins, HarperPerennial ed., 1994), 272–279.
3. My discussion of the Glorious Revolution is based upon my general knowledge of the subject, supported by information in Churchill, The New World, 383–410.

II. WE THE PEOPLE

Washington Crosses the Delaware

1. This phraseology is based on the celebrated comment by the British Prime Minister Sir Robert Walpole who said, as London's churches rang their bells at the start of a war, "They are ringing their bells now, but soon they will be wringing their hands." Churchill, Age of Revolution, 122.
2. Churchill, Age of Revolution, 190.
3. Barbara Tuchman, The Guns of August (New York: Macmillan, 1962; New York: Dell Publishing Co., Dell Contemporary Classic 1971), 485, quoting General Kluck.

Valley Forge

1. This challenge came in a commencement speech by Churchill at the Harrow School.
2. Mrs. Charles Ellis (wife of the pastor) often made this point in the adult Sunday School class at Clarkson Community Church.
3. The spacecraft was the Mars Climate Orbiter in 1999.

Yorktown

1. My discussion of George Washington is based upon my general knowledge of the subject, supported by information in James Thomas Flexner, Washington: The Indispensable Man (New York: Little, Brown and Company 1974).

Washington Sends the Army Home
1. See David McCullough, Truman (New York: Simon & Schuster 1992), 470.
2. My account of this crisis is based upon my general knowledge of the subject, supported by information in Flexner, Washington: The Indispensable Man, 169–178.

The Constitution
1. See 1 Chronicles 12:32, referring to those "who understood the times and knew what Israel should do."
2. Barck and Lefler, Colonial America, page 682, and Flexner, Washington: The Indispensable Man, page177.
3. My discussion of the problems that led to the calling of the Constitutional Convention is based upon my general knowledge of the subject, supported by information in Barck and Lefler, Colonial America, 662–676, and Flexner, Washington: The Indispensable Man, 197–203.
4. My discussion of the Constitutional Convention is based upon my general knowledge of the subject, supported by information in Barck and Lefler, Colonial America, 685–691, and Flexner, Washington: The Indispensable Man, 204–209.
5. Stephen B. Oates, With Malice Toward None: A Life of Abraham Lincoln (New York: Harper & Row, 1977; New York: HarperPerennial, 1994), 112–13.
6. My account of "Washington and Slavery" draws upon my general knowledge of the subject, supported by information in the chapter with that name in Flexner, Washington: The Indispensable Man, 385–94.
7. Flexner, Washington: The Indispensable Man, 386.
8. Flexner, Washington: The Indispensable Man, 386–87.
9. According to John Bartlett, Bartlett's Familiar Quotations, 14th ed., edited by Emily Morison Beck (Boston: Little, Brown 1968), 486, Henry Lee, known as Light-Horse Harry, drafted this resolution that was adopted by the House of Representatives in December 1799 upon the death of Washington.

George Washington Becomes President
1. Flexner, Washington: The Indispensable Man, 256.
2. Flexner, Washington: The Indispensable Man, 385–86.
3. Flexner, Washington: The Indispensable Man, 387.
4. Lerone Bennett, Jr., Before the Mayflower: A History of Black America, 6th ed. (New York: Penguin Books 1993), 85.

The Louisiana Purchase

1. Flexner, Washington: The Indispensable Man, 198, 252, 253. Barck and Lefler, Colonial America, 674–76, 682–83.
2. Stephen E. Ambrose, Undaunted Courage: Meriwether Lewis, Thomas Jefferson, and the Opening of the American West (New York: Simon & Schuster, Touchstone 1997), 51–52, 56.
3. David Herbert Donald, Lincoln (New York: Simon & Schuster, Touchstone 1996), 34–35; 38–39.
4. Ambrose, Undaunted Courage, 72.
5. Ambrose, Undaunted Courage, 101.
6. Randall, Thomas Jefferson: A Life, 567.
7. Ambrose, Undaunted Courage, 72, 101; Randall, Thomas Jefferson: A Life, 565–66; Bennett, Before the Mayflower, 124–25. My discussion of events in Haiti is based upon my general knowledge of the subject, supported by information in Bennett, Before the Mayflower, 112–25.
8. Ambrose, Undaunted Courage, 56.
9. Notes on the State of Virginia [1781–1785], 19, according to Bartlett, Bartlett's Familiar Quotations, 471.
10. I discuss these ideas at greater length in the chapter of my upcoming book, The Rises and Falls of Ancient Israelites, that is titled "Elijah Condemns Jezebel For Killing Naboth so that Ahab Could Take His Vineyard." My ideas on this subject were stimulated by comments from Professor Lance Liebman in my first year Property course at Harvard Law School when he taught us Charles Reich's ideas about "The New Property."

The Lewis and Clark Expedition

1. Ambrose, Undaunted Courage, 75. My account of the Lewis and Clark expedition is based on my general knowledge of the subject, supported by information in Ambrose, Undaunted Courage.

III. THE LAST, BEST HOPE OF HUMANITY

The Cotton Gin and the Erie Canal

1. My account of the Civil War and Reconstruction era in America is based on my general knowledge of the subject, supported by information in J.G. Randall and David Herbert Donald, The Civil War and Reconstruction, 2d ed. (Lexington, Mass.: D.C. Heath and Company, 1969) and the other resource materials listed in these notes.
2. Winston S. Churchill, The Great Democracies, Vol. 4 of History of the English-Speaking Peoples, 136.

3. Letter to John Holmes on April 22, 1820, according to Bartlett, Bartlett's Familiar Quotations, 473.
4. Letter to John Adams on September 12, 1821, according to Bartlett, Bartlett's Familiar Quotations, 473.
5. Lincoln's Second Annual Message to Congress on December 1, 1862, according to Bartlett, Bartlett's Familiar Quotations, 638.

Frederick Douglass and Harriett Beecher Stowe

1. Flexner, Washington: The Indispensable Man, 198 (emphasis in the original).
2. Frederick Douglass, Narrative of the Life of Frederick Douglass: An American Slave, ed. Benjamin Quarles (1845; reprint, Cambridge, Mass.: Harvard University Press, Belknap Press, 1988). A longer autobiographical work that contains much of the same material is Frederick Douglass, My Bondage and My Freedom (1855; reprint, New York: Dover Publications, 1969).
3. Douglass, Narrative of the Life, 56.
4. Douglass, Narrative of the Life, 66 (emphasis in original).
5. Douglass, Narrative of the Life, 58.
6. Douglass, Narrative of the Life, 58–59.
7. Douglass, Narrative of the Life, 59.
8. Bennett, Before the Mayflower, 160.
9. The quotations from this speech are taken from Douglass, My Bondage and My Freedom, 441–45 (emphasis in original).

Sojourner Truth and Harriett Tubman

1. Frederick Douglass spoke these words in his speech at the West India Emancipation Celebration at Canandaigua, New York on August 4, 1857, as reported in Bennett, Before the Mayflower, 160–61.
2. Bennett, Before the Mayflower, 166.
3. My discussion of Sojourner Truth and Harriett Tubman is based upon my general knowledge of the subject, supported by information in and quotations from Bennett, Before the Mayflower, 163–67 (emphasis in original).

Abraham Lincoln versus Stephen Douglas

1. Donald, Lincoln, 214–15, 237–38.
2. Donald, Lincoln, 61, 84, 214–15.
3. Oates, With Malice Toward None, 4.
4. This was a quote from Gray's Elegy. Donald, Lincoln, 19.
5. Donald, Lincoln, 215.
6. Donald, Lincoln, 215.
7. Benjamin P. Thomas, Abraham Lincoln (1952; reprint, New York: Barnes & Noble 1994), 153. Although these remarks by Herndon referred specifi-

Visions of America, Visions of the Church

cally to Lincoln's efforts to have the Illinois legislature elect him to the U.S. Senate after the 1854 elections, I feel that they accurately convey the persistence in the face of setbacks that epitomized Lincoln's life.

8. Donald, Lincoln, 61.

9. My discussion of Lincoln's political career is based upon my general knowledge of the subject, supported by information in the biographies of Lincoln that are referenced in other notes.

10. Although business (and the slow means of transportation in those days before cars and jetliners) often kept them apart, and although they often quarreled, "they were devoted to each other. In the long years of their marriage Abraham Lincoln was never suspected of being unfaithful to his wife. She, in turn, was immensely proud of him and was his most loyal supporter and admirer." Donald, Lincoln, 108.

11. Donald, Lincoln, 85.

12. Donald, Lincoln, 108.

13. Donald, Lincoln, at 163.

14. Barck and Lefler, Colonial America, 681.

15. Randall and Donald, The Civil War, 121.

16. Donald, Lincoln, 168.

17. Donald, Lincoln, 170.

18. Donald, Lincoln, 170.

19. Donald, Lincoln, 174–77.

20. Donald, Lincoln, 192.

21. Donald, Lincoln, 192 (emphasis in original).

22. Bartlett, Bartlett's Familiar Quotations, 547 (emphasis added).

Fort Sumter

1. Oates, With Malice Toward None, 161,177.

2. Donald, Lincoln, 206–07,209,236; Oates, With Malice Toward None, 142.

3. Donald, Lincoln, 246.

4. Donald, Lincoln, 269.

5. Donald, Lincoln, 244.

6. Randall and Donald, The Civil War, 133.

7. Lincoln received about one million fewer votes than all three of his major opponents combined. However, Lincoln would have won the election in the Electoral College even if he had run against only one candidate (instead of the three arrayed against him) because he still would have carried enough large states to win by 35 votes in the Electoral College. Donald, Lincoln, 133–34.

8. For example, the infamous Dred Scott decision in 1857 was premised on the Supreme Court's conclusion that black people were not citizens protected by the U.S. Constitution. Furthermore, from the racist perspective of the Supreme Court, it was self-evident that black people were not "cre-

ated equal" to white people, and that, therefore, black people did not have any unalienable rights such as life, liberty, and the pursuit of happiness. (Notice the striking parallels with the Supreme Court's decision in Roe v. Wade, where the Supreme Court's decision was premised on its conclusion that unborn babies are not people protected by the U.S. Constitution and that unborn babies are not people whose right to life is guaranteed by the Declaration of Independence.)

A primary tenet of the Republican Party was that the Dred Scott decision must be overturned. It was, but only after the fathomless suffering of the Civil War. In 1868, the Fourteenth Amendment was added to the Constitution, declaring that "[a]ll persons born . . . in the United States . . . are citizens of the United States," and that no State shall "deprive any person of life, liberty, or property . . . nor deny to any person . . . the equal protection of the laws."

9. Randall and Donald, The Civil War, 125–26,166.
10. Donald, Lincoln, 260.
11. Randall and Donald, The Civil War, 166–69,187n.1.
12. Donald, Lincoln, 273.
13. Donald, Lincoln, 236, 257.
14. Donald, Lincoln, 24, 30–31, 273.
15. Randall and Donald, The Civil War, 164.
16. Donald, Lincoln, 594. Lincoln was fatally wounded by a shot to the head on Good Friday. He never regained consciousness and he stopped breathing the next day.
17. Donald, Lincoln, 284.
18. Donald, Lincoln, 285.
19. Donald, Lincoln, 268–270.
20. Barck and Lefler, Colonial America, 690.
21. Donald, Lincoln, 269–70.
22. Bennett, Before the Mayflower, 185.
23. Bennett, Before the Mayflower, 186.
24. Thomas, Abraham Lincoln, 255–56.
25. Donald, Lincoln, 292.
26. Donald, Lincoln, 295–97.
27. Thomas, Abraham Lincoln, 257–59; Donald, Lincoln, 296; Oates, With Malice Toward None, 226.
28. Bennett, Before the Mayflower, 186.

Abraham Lincoln versus George McClellan
1. Churchill, The Great Democracies, 177.
2. Bruce Catton, This Hallowed Ground: The Story of the Union Side of the Civil War (Garden City, New York: Doubleday, 1956; New York: Simon &

Schuster, Pocket Cardinal, 1960), 54–58; Churchill, The Great Democracies, 178–180.

3. Churchill, The Great Democracies, 189; Randall and Donald, The Civil War, 201.
4. Randall and Donald, The Civil War, 196–97.
5. Donald, Lincoln, 318–20.
6. Donald, Lincoln, 369.
7. Donald, Lincoln, 349; Catton, This Hallowed Ground, 167–68.
8. Donald, Lincoln, 329–31.
9. Donald, Lincoln, 338–41.
10. Donald, Lincoln, 339–42.
11. Donald, Lincoln, 356–57.
12. Catton, This Hallowed Ground, 164–65, 167.
13. Bruce Catton, The Army of the Potomac: Mr. Lincoln's Army (Garden City, New York: Doubleday 1951), 123.
14. Churchill, The Great Democracies, 181, 190, 195.
15. Churchill, The Great Democracies, 199–200, 204–09.
16. Bartlett, Bartlett's Familiar Quotations, 547.
17. Randall and Donald, The Civil War, 219.
18. Catton, This Hallowed Ground, 195–96.
19. Catton, This Hallowed Ground, 202–03; Catton, Mr. Lincoln's Army, 319.
20. Catton, This Hallowed Ground, 206–07, 210; Donald, Lincoln, 385–86.
21. Donald, Lincoln, 389.
22. Donald, Lincoln, 389–90.
23. Catton, This Hallowed Ground, 192–94.
24. Churchill, The Great Democracies, 217. The speaker was William Gladstone, at that time the Chancellor of the Exchequer, who subsequently became one of Britain's greatest Prime Ministers. Although his speech came after the battle of Antietam, it accurately reflected the Prime Minister's views prior to the Union victory at Antietam and Lincoln's Emancipation Proclamation because Gladstone made the speech before learning that the Prime Minister, Palmerston, had changed his mind about mediating an end to the war.
25. Donald, Lincoln, 365–66; Randall and Donald, The Civil War, 376–79.

Abraham Lincoln versus Robert E. Lee

1. Randall and Donald, The Civil War, 215.
2. Randall and Donald, The Civil War, 215.
3. Randall and Donald, The Civil War, 224–25.
4. Randall and Donald, The Civil War, 379–83.
5. Donald, Lincoln, 377.
6. Bennett, Before the Mayflower, 197.
7. Bennett, Before the Mayflower, 199.

8. Bennett, Before the Mayflower, 198–99.
9. For stirring accounts of the Battles of Chancellorsville and Gettysburg, no one surpasses Winston Churchill in The Great Democracies, 223–30.
10. Churchill, The Great Democracies, 241.
11. Churchill, The Great Democracies, 239–40.
12. Bruce Catton, The Army of the Potomac: A Stillness at Appomattox (Garden City, New York: Doubleday, 1953), 288–89.
13. Bruce Catton, A Stillness at Appomattox, 294–95.
14. Donald, Lincoln, 108.
15. Catton, This Hallowed Ground, 475–76.
16. Donald, Lincoln, 284.

IV. PEACE FOR ALL HUMANITY

The Election of 1876
1. Republican apologists have argued, however, that the Republican candidate would have had more votes cast for him if groups such as the Ku Klux Klan had not intimidated so many blacks and kept them from voting. Randall and Donald, The Civil War, 687–91. As Randall and Donald summarized the historians' conundrum (691, n.1): "It is impossible to arrive at even a fairly satisfactory conclusion as to the votes of these [disputed] states, the problem being how far Democratic intimidation offset Republican fraud."
2. Douglass, My Bondage and My Freedom, 398–99.
3. Donald, Lincoln, 165–67.
4. Bennett, Before the Mayflower, 181.
5. Bennett, Before the Mayflower, 198–99.

"Lafayette, We Are Here"
1. Oscar Theodore Barck, Jr. and Nelson Manfred Blake, Since 1900: A History of the United States in Our Times, 5th ed. (New York: Macmillan, 1974), 148.
2. Churchill, The Great Democracies, 329–30.
3. Tuchman, Guns of August, 356.
4. Tuchman, Guns of August, 196.
5. Barck and Blake, Since 1900, 153.
6. Newspapers attributed the words to the leader of the American Expeditionary Force, General Pershing, but he said that the words were spoken by one of his aides, Colonel Charles E. Stanton. Don Lawson, The United States in World War I (New York: Scholastic Magazines, Scholastic Books Services, 1964), 6.

Hakuna Matata

1. Simba, Pumba and Timon sing about their problem-free philosophy in the song "Hakuna Matata." Music by Elton John. Lyrics by Tim Rice. Copyright 1994 Walt Disney Music Company (ASCAP).

Raising The Star-Spangled Banner

1. This phrase was the title of a famous love song by The Carpenters that was often played at weddings in the 1970s: "We've Only Just Begun."

The Buck Stops Here

1. This maxim of the Victorian Age's sense of duty and optimism is set forth in poetic form in Black Beauty by Anne Sewell.

The New Frontier

1. Bartlett, Bartlett's Familiar Quotations, 1072.

The Cuban Missile Crisis

1. Robert F. Kennedy, Thirteen Days: A Memoir of the Cuban Missile Crisis (New York: W.W. Norton & Company, 1969; New York: New American Library, Signet Books, 1969), 25–27, 107–08.
2. Kennedy, Thirteen Days, 62–63, 127.
3. Kennedy, Thirteen Days, 69–71.
4. Kennedy, Thirteen Days, 72.

The Assassination of Martin Luther King

1. David J. Garrow, Bearing the Cross: Martin Luther King, Jr., and the Southern Christian Leadership Conference (New York: William Morrow and Company, 1986; New York: Quill 1999), 283.
2. Garrow, Bearing the Cross, 283–84.
3. Garrow, Bearing the Cross, 620–21.

The Assassination of Bobby Kennedy

1. Bobby Kennedy credited the great playwright, George Bernard Shaw, for coming up with these words that Bobby Kennedy made into the theme of his ill-fated campaign.

Apollo 8

1. Chaikin, Man on the Moon, 121–22 (emphasis in original). A black and white copy of the photograph showing "earthrise" is in the photos following page 238.

Apollo 11

1. The full quote reads:
    HERE MEN FROM THE PLANET EARTH
    FIRST SET FOOT UPON THE MOON
    JULY 1969, A.D.
    WE CAME IN PEACE FOR ALL MANKIND
2. Chaikin, Man on the Moon, 208–15.

Only Nixon Could Go To China

1. The announcement that "peace is at hand" came from Henry Kissinger (who was leading the negotiations) just twelve days before the election. Thomas A. Bailey, David M. Kennedy, Lizabeth Cohen, The American Pageant: A History of the Republic, 11th ed. (Boston: Houghton Mifflin, 1998), 972. I remember Kissinger's announcement, as well as Nixon's emphatic assurances on the evening before the election.

Saint Jimmy

1. See the picture in Bailey, Kennedy and Cohen, American Pageant, 981.

BOOK TWO: VISIONS OF THE CHURCH

I. GETTING OFF THE LAUNCH PAD

1. Chaikin, Man on the Moon, 80.
2. Jim Lovell and Jeffrey Kluger, Apollo 13 (New York: Simon & Schuster, Pocket Books, 1995; motion picture screenplay by William Broyles, Jr. and Al Reinert), 171. Lovell and Kluger, Apollo 13 was previously titled Lost Moon: The Perilous Voyage of Apollo 13 (New York Houghton Mifflin, 1994).

II. REACHING ORBIT

1. See Acts 21:17–26. W.H.C. Frend, The Rise of Christianity (Philadelphia: Fortress Press, 1984, 257; David Chidester, Christianity: A Global History (New York: HarperCollins, 2000), 31–33; Owen Chadwick, A History of Christianity (New York: St. Martin's Press, 1995), 15; Kenneth Scott Latourette, Beginnings to 1500, vol. 1 of A History of Christianity, rev. ed.

(New York: HarperCollins, 1975), at 120–122. Volume 1 contains through page 683 of the hardcover edition of Latourette, A History of Christianity.

III. PREPARING THE SPACESHIP TO LEAVE EARTH'S ORBIT

The Universal Church Councils

1. This version of the Nicene Creed is taken from The Hymnal of the Free Methodist Church, published by special arrangement with Word Music, The Hymnal: For Worship and Celebration (Irving, Texas: Word Music, 1989), Reading 717. "It will be noted that the creed which today bears the name of Nicene is a further development from the one which was adopted at Nicaea. Yet the latter's essential features were preserved." Latourette, History of Christianity, 156.

   An English translation of the Creed of Nicaea found on page 499 of Frend, Rise of Christianity, reads as follows:

   We believe in one God the Father All—sovereign, maker of all things visible and invisible; and in one Lord Jesus Christ, the Son of God, begotten of the Father, only-begotten, that is the substance of the Father, God of God, Light of Light, true God of true God, by whom all things were made, things in heaven and things on the earth; who for us men and for our salvation came down and was made flesh, and became man, suffered, and rose on the third day, ascended into heaven, and is coming to judge the living and the dead. And in the Holy Spirit. And those that say, "There was when he was not," and "Before he was begotten he was not," and that, "He came into being from what-is-not," or those that allege, that the Son of God is "of another substance or essence" or "created" or "changeable" or "alterable," these the Catholic and Apostolic Church anathematizes.

2. My discussion of the Universal Church Councils is based upon my general knowledge of the subject, supported by information in Frend, Rise of Christianity and Latourette, History of Christianity.

3. Frend, Rise of Christianity, 755, 771.

4. Frend, Rise of Christianity, 772.

5. Portions of my upcoming book, Hoping in the Lord: The Messiah, describe Jesus blessing children, welcoming sinners, weeping with those who weep, and washing the feet of those in need.

6. This is a twist to the title of the long-running soap opera that my mother used to love to watch when I was a little boy: "As the World Turns." As an example of how much "family values" have declined in the past forty years since my mother watched the show, it is worth noting that my mother stopped watching the show because one of the characters was going to get a divorce and my mother didn't want me to learn about such a terrible

thing. She thought that it would upset me too much if I learned that mothers and fathers sometimes split up.

7. Roberto Unger, who taught me jurisprudence at Harvard Law School, stressed the importance of attaining a philosophy of Law and of Life in which the grandest themes and purposes of Law and Life could be experienced in the smallest, most routine details of our daily lives.

8. For example, Jesus frequently poked fun at those who disagreed with him. (Matthew 16:2–3; Mark 12:37–39; Luke 12:16–20; John 8:7–9) and Jesus must have joined in the laughter at parties such as the wedding at Cana. (John 2:1–11).

St. Augustine

1. My discussion of St. Augustine is based upon my general knowledge of the subject, supported by information in Chidester, Christianity: A Global History, 125–140; Latourette, History of Christianity, 96–97, 173–181; and Peter Brown, Augustine of Hippo: A Biography new ed. (London: Faber and Faber, 1967; Berkley and Los Angeles: University of California Press), St. Augustine, Confessions, trans. and introduction by R.S. Pine-Coffin, Penguin Classics (New York: Penguin Putnam, 1961); and St. Augustine, The City of God, trans. Marcus Dods, The Modern Library (with an introduction by Thomas Merton, New York: Random House, 1950).

2. St. Augustine, Confessions, 177–78 (the end of Book VIII). The verse quoted by St. Augustine is a portion of Romans 13:13–14 (emphasis in original).

3. These verses of "Amazing Grace" were written by John Newton.

4. St. Augustine, City of God, 866 (near end of Book XXII).

5. St. Augustine, City of God, 859 (Book XXII, 29)

6. St. Augustine, City of God, 867 (near end of Book XXII)

7. This final verse of "Amazing Grace" was written by John P. Rees.

IV. "HOUSTON, WE'VE HAD A PROBLEM"

1. Chaikin, Man On the Moon, 292–296.

Who Is the Greatest?

1. A portion of my upcoming book, Rises and Falls of Ancient Israelites, discusses the need for Christians to be "best friends" like Jonathan and David were and sets forth the long, lamentable catalogue of sins that Christians have committed against each other over the past two thousand years. That discussion complements Visions of the Church.

2. Latourette, History of Christianity, 411–12.

3. Latourette, History of Christianity, 412.

V. Relying Upon the Lunar Module
1. Chidester, Christianity: A Global History, 262.
2. Chidester, Christianity: A Global History, 283.
3. Some verses from "All Creatures of Our God and King."

VI. Flying the Spaceship

The Unknown Christians
1. Sainte-Chapelle was built in the 13th century. The king who ordered Sainte-Chapelle built was Louis IX (St. Louis). He lived from 1214–1270. Aquinas lived from 1225(?)–1274.

St. Thomas Aquinas
1. Aquinas, Summa of Theology III, q. 26, a 1,c and III, q. 48, a.2, c. as set forth in Mary T. Clark, ed., An Aquinas Reader: Selections from the Writings of Thomas Aquinas, introduction by Mary T. Clark (1972; reprinted by special arrangement with Image Books/Doubleday, New York: Fordham Press, 1988), 468–69. My discussion of St. Thomas Aquinas is based upon my general knowledge of the subject, supported by information in Clark, An Aquinas Reader.
2. Aquinas, Summa of Christian Teaching IV, 22 as set forth in Clark, Aquinas Reader, 301.

Martin Luther
1. Latourette, History of Christianity, 706–07.
2. Chidester, Christianity: A Global History, 313.

John Wesley
1. John Wesley, The Journal of John Wesley, ed. Percy Livingstone Parker (Chicago: Moody Press, 1952), 64 (the entry for Wednesday, May 24, 1738).

VII. Resurrecting the Command Module

1. Lovell and Kluger, Apollo 13, 235.
2. Lovell and Kluger, Apollo 13, 379–380.

Martin Luther King, Jr.: Hope
1. Garrow, Bearing the Cross: Martin Luther King, 621.

Mother Teresa: Love

1. Becky Benenate and Joseph Durepos, eds., Mother Teresa: No Greater Love (published by arrangement with New World Library, New York: Fine Creative Media, MJF Books, 1997), 22–23. Benenate and Durepos, Mother Teresa: No Greater Love was originally published as The Mother Teresa Reader, A Life for God, compiled by LaVonne Neff and published by Servant Publications in 1995.

2. In this book full of insights from the flight of Apollo 13, it is fitting that the reference to this key verse about faith, hope, and love (referring to I Corinthians, Chapter 13, Verse 13) repeats the number "13" twice!

VIII. Reaching Home

1. Chaikin, Man on the Moon, 128.

How to Order the General Counsel Series

As a "war of civilizations" threatens Humanity, read the following books of the General Counsel Series to discover the civilization that is good, that is very good—the Promised Land:

The Promised Land (Vol. 1) draws upon high points of the Bible—from Genesis through Ruth—to teach us how to find the Promised Land, how to establish the work of our hands, and how to be strong and courageous.

Healing the Promised Land (Vol. 2) draws upon high points of the Bible—from the rise of the Monarchy in Ancient Israel to the renewal of Jerusalem after the Babylonian Exile—to teach us how to heal our personal Promised Lands and how to heal God's Promised Land.

Hoping in the LORD (Vol. 3) draws upon high points of the Bible—from Matthew to John—to teach us how Jesus carries us to the Promised Land.

Lighting the World (Vol. 4) draws upon high points of the Bible—from Acts through Revelation—to teach us how to light the world, not by might, nor by power, but by God's Spirit so that we reach the Promised Land.

Visions of America, Visions of the Church (Vol. 5) draws upon high points of American and Church history to teach us how Humanity can find peace and joy in the Promised Land.

Each volume of the General Counsel Series is available online at amazon.com and barnesandnoble.com

CPSIA information can be obtained
at www.ICGtesting.com
Printed in the USA
BVOW03s1101050217
475342BV00001B/28/P